PSYCHIATRIC DISORDERS OF CHILDREN WITH CONGENITAL RUBELLA

Psychiatric Disorders
of
Children with
Congenital Rubella

STELLA CHESS, M.D.

Professor of Child Psychiatry
New York University Medical Center

SAM J. KORN, Ph.D.

Associate Professor, Department of Psychology
Hunter College, City University of New York

PAULINA B. FERNANDEZ, Ph.D.

Senior Clinical Psychologist
New York University Medical Center

BRUNNER/MAZEL • New York
BUTTERWORTHS • London

Copyright © 1971 by Brunner/Mazel, Inc.
Published by BRUNNER/MAZEL, INC.
64 University Place, New York, N. Y. 10003

Library of Congress Catalogue Card No. 71-173092
SBN 87630-046-8

MANUFACTURED IN THE UNITED STATES OF AMERICA

ACKNOWLEDGMENTS

THE INITIAL IMPETUS for this research came from Drs. Saul Krugman and Louis Cooper of New York University Medical Center who stimulated our interest in studying the behavioral organization of children in their Rubella Birth Defect Evaluation Project.* We would like to thank them and their staff for acting as liaison with the parents and making available data on the children's physical status. We are also grateful to the parents and their youngsters who cooperated with us and made this study possible.

The research reported herein was supported by the Children's Bureau, Department of Health, Education, and Welfare under Grant H 220 (C2).

Many individuals assisted in this research, and we would like to thank in particular Dr. John Donohue, staff psychiatrist, Becky Adelson, social worker, and Ligia Sainz, translator, for their participation. Research assistants and interviewers to whom we also owe our gratitude are Beatrice Hyman, Ruth Sinreich, Lillian Klein, Sylvia Zuckerman, and Richard Sinreich. Thanks, too, to Linda Rich and other secretaries for their many contributions.

Special appreciation is due Abby Hand, our editorial associate, for her participation throughout the preparation of this book and to Samuel Sillen for his review of the final manuscript.

Chapter 9 represents an expansion of a previously published paper, "Autism in Children with Congenital Rubella," which appeared in the *Journal of Autism and Childhood Schizophrenia*, 1: 33-47, 1971. Appreciation is extended to this *Journal* for permission to incorporate portions of this paper in the present volume.

* The RBDEP has been supported by grants from the National Foundation—March of Dimes and the National Institute of Allergy and Infectious Disease.

TABLE OF CONTENTS

INTRODUCTION

IN 1941, Sir Norman McAlister Gregg of Australia called attention to the etiologic relationship between rubella and congenital defects. Although the disease had been first described in the early 18th century and its viral nature established by the late 1930's, it was not until Gregg's report on congenital cataracts in infants born of mothers infected during early pregnancy that rubella received the attention warranted by its clinical and public health importance.

In the past thirty years, evidence has accumulated on the far-reaching damage that may occur in the fetus, even if the mother's infection has been quite benign. Originally, the "rubella syndrome" included only cataracts, congenital heart defect, and deafness. Recent research, however, has indicated that the consequences of fetal infection are much more diverse. Possible impairments range from incapacitating physical and intellectual handicaps to subtle behavioral anomalies.

The 1964 epidemic of rubella in the United States left in its wake an estimated 20,000 children with congenital malformations. In order to study and provide services for children in the New York area whose mothers were suspected of having had rubella during pregnancy, a multidisciplinary Rubella Birth Defect Evaluation Project was established at New York University Medical Center. Its aim was to examine the clinical manifestations of the disease and to develop appropriate management techniques. In conjunction with this project, one of us (S.C.) undertook a behavioral study, supported by the Children's Bureau of the Department of Health, Education, and Welfare, to determine the psychological and psychiatric sequelae of congenital rubella. The study encompassed both the children and their families.

The rationale for this behavioral study was the fact that the various physical defects caused by rubella had immediate and striking effects on the child's and parent's behavior. We sought to evaluate the youngsters and their families with regard to specific aspects of their psychological functioning and to advise parents on ways of handling the children. By identifying the special behavioral and intellectual consequences of congenital rubella, we hoped to throw light on the best way of treating and educating these children.

We began studying the 243 youngsters in our sample when they were approximately two and a half to four years of age. Developmental research has established the decisive nature of a child's experiences and stimulation before the age of five. Therefore, it was crucial to analyze the behavior of a rubella child as early as possible in order to determine the extent of his handicaps, the degree to which they interfered with his ability to make contact with the world, and the optimal course of remediation. This was particularly important since so many of the rubella children have sensory defects. We were interested in determining the effects of diminished sensorial input on a youngster's intellectual development and overall ability to interact with others. Although studies of the deaf have elucidated some of these problems, they were insufficient, since our children frequently had multiple defects. The parents' role as mediator, crucial in facilitating the contact of any young child with the world, is all the more important when the child has sensory and other handicaps that can interfere with his living a happy and meaningful life.

Family studies were also important in this group of children, in part because of the unique nature of the disease process. Very often, the mother had had only some minor discomfort (or even none at all) when she contracted rubella during pregnancy and suddenly, when the child was born, was confronted with overwhelming problems in caring for him. While these difficulties are inherent in the care of any multihandicapped child, the fact that the mother may feel responsible for the child's defects must be dealt with insofar as it affects the way she handles him.

Although the scope of this study has not yet permitted longitudinal research, it will be important to do follow-up studies of these rubella children. Many of the signs that now show up as subtle behavior deviations may well become full-blown problems when the child must respond to the academic demands and other exigencies of school life. Furthermore, the social impact of the child's handicaps may become increasingly important to his behavioral development as he grows older and goes out into a world organized primarily for "normal" children.

This is the first detailed study of the behavioral consequences of congenital rubella in such a large group of children. Obviously, the results of our investigation are most pertinent to the rubella children born after the 1964 epidemic and their parents and teachers. With the development of the rubella vaccine and the adoption of liberalized abortion laws, it is likely that the number of infants born in the United States with rubella will greatly decline in years to come. Nevertheless, because rubella remains endemic in other parts of the world, we hope that our findings can be generalized to these other populations. Finally, although the defects in our study youngsters have a specific etiology, their consequences may be relevant in working with other multihandicapped children who demand similar understanding and comparable services.

PSYCHIATRIC DISORDERS OF CHILDREN WITH CONGENITAL RUBELLA

1

Rubella: The Research Background

THE FIRST DESCRIPTIONS of rubella appear in the medical literature of the early 18th century (Forbes, 1969). During the following 150 years, interest focused on refining its clinical identity and establishing it as a discrete diagnostic category "similar in some respects to but not identical with either measles or scarlatina" (West, 1881).

For almost half of this century, rubella was considered a mild and comparatively unimportant infectious disease of childhood. Although it was often characterized by a rash, adenopathy, fever, and headache, complications rarely occurred and, in many cases, the infection went undetected as it caused no manifestations or complaints. Even when adults contracted rubella, they frequently had few or no symptoms of the disease. (It was not until the

1

isolation of rubella virus in tissue culture and techniques for serologic diagnosis were described [Parkman et al., 1962; Weller and Neva, 1962] that these subclinical cases would be identified.)

The modern era of rubella research began in 1941 when Gregg reported an "epidemic" of congenital cataracts in infants whose mothers had rubella in early pregnancy. His observations focused attention on the devastating effects of the virus on the developing fetus and indicated the need for studying congenital rubella and the rubella syndrome.

Since Gregg's original discovery of the teratogenic role of rubella virus, the mechanism by which malformations are produced has been elucidated. The virus travels through the mother's bloodstream to the placenta and then to the fetus (Dudgeon, 1969). Several investigators have recovered virus from fetal tissues obtained at therapeutic abortion (Kay et al., 1964; Heggie and Weir, 1964) as well as from the tissues, urine, and nasopharynx of live-born infants (Alford et al., 1964; Horstmann et al., 1965; Korones et al., 1967; Phillips et al., 1965). Other studies indicate that children with congenital rubella may excrete virus from birth to at least 18 months of age (Butler et al., 1965; Blattner, 1966; Cooper and Krugman, 1966; Lambert et al., 1965). These recovery reports point out the widespread dissemination of the virus as well as the chronic and persistent nature of the infection.

It is generally accepted that the malformations seen in congenital rubella result from cell death or a change in the rate of cell growth. In addition, damage may be caused by interference with the blood supply to developing fetal tissues. In vitro studies have shown that "human cells derived from any organ can be infected with rubella virus" (Plotkin et al., 1967). When the cells are infected in utero, there may be "slower growth and limited doubling potential in the daughter cells. Inhibition of cell multiplication, in turn, may result in retarded growth and anomalous development of the heart, eye, ear and other organs" (Singer et al., 1967). The defects found, therefore, may be "interpreted as interrupted, retarded or disorganized maturation of tissue"

(Singer *et al.*, 1967). Furthermore, the "variety of defects . . . suggests that the congenital rubella syndrome is an expression of generalized viral invasion and persistent multiplication of the agent in the tissues" (Lindquist *et al.*, 1965).

Although the incidence of malformation due to congenital rubella varies from one study to another, most investigators agree that the effect on the fetus can be correlated with the timing of the maternal infection. Malformations are most prominent following infection in the first trimester, especially the first two months of pregnancy, and estimates of their incidence vary from 10 to 50%. However, fetal damage may occur following infection later in pregnancy, and has even been reported when the mother had rubella prior to conception (Cooper *et al.*, 1969; Hardy *et al.*, 1969; Lundstrom, 1962; Sever *et al.*, 1969).

The insidiousness of the disease becomes even more apparent when it is realized that the damage done to the fetus bears no correlation to the severity of the disease in the mother. Although it was first thought that fetal effects occurred only when the mother had overt signs of rubella, it is now known that a pregnant woman who has no obvious infection at all may still give birth to a damaged child (Avery *et al.*, 1965).

Following Gregg's identification of congenital cataracts in rubella infants (he also noted low birth weight, feeding difficulties, and congenital heart disease, but did not emphasize these findings), Swan presented a report (1943) describing deafness and delayed speech development as other sequelae. Gregg in 1945 added mental retardation, deaf-mutism, microphthalmos, and dental defects to this growing list of abnormalities. Beginning with the report of Lundstrom (1962), who described the aftermath of a Swedish epidemic, and continuing through those of many investigators studying the 1964 epidemic in the United States, a whole host of malformations and defects have been associated with children whose mothers had rubella during pregnancy.

Thus, though deafness, cataracts, and congenital heart disease were for many years considered the congenital rubella syn-

drome, this triad has now been expanded to include defects ranging from the most obvious and severe to the most subtle, with
hardly a body organ or system left untouched by the virus. A list
of the more common symptoms of congenital rubella, therefore,
must now also include low birth weight and delayed neonatal
growth (Cooper *et al.,* 1969; Horstmann *et al.,* 1965; Lambert,
1965; Swan *et al.,* 1945), thrombocytopenic purpura (Cooper *et
al.,* 1965; Desmond *et al.,* 1970; Plotkin *et al.,* 1967), transient
bone lesions (Korones *et al.,* 1967; Plotkin *et al.,* 1967), anemia,
hepatitis (Cooper *et al.,* 1969), microcephaly (Dekaban and
O'Rourke, 1958; Hardy *et al.,* 1966; Michaels and Kenny, 1969;
Plotkin *et al.,* 1967), psychomotor retardation (Lundstrom, 1962;
Michaels and Kenny, 1969), and other disorders, all of which are
now subsumed under the diagnosis "expanded rubella syndrome"
(*British Medical Journal,* 1965). The "incidence of these newly
recognized and severe manifestations of congenital rubella is probably attributed to . . . the enormity and extent of one of the
largest epidemics of rubella in the history of the United States;
the availability and use of rubella virus isolation procedures for
the diagnosis of suspect cases of congenital rubella; and the rapid
dissemination of scientific information by a barrage of medical
and lay publications" (Krugman, 1965).

At first, the failure to associate the new features of the expanded syndrome with fetal rubella caused investigators to postulate a supervirulent virus hypothesis. However, when substanti-
ated cases of congenital rubella prior to 1964 were examined,
clinical features were found in the infants that were similar to
those found following the 1964 epidemic. Most researchers now
conclude, therefore, that the "infrequency with which such infants are seen during nonepidemic years and . . . the pre-1964
misconception of the congenital rubella syndrome as a condition
of static, structural abnormalities rather than a continuing, infectious disease" (White *et al.,* 1969) led to the suggestion of a supervirulent strain but that there is no substantial proof of this.

In addition, these newer studies indicate that damage may be done in the neonatal period, due to the ongoing nature of the infection, and that there may be "active postnatal (in addition to prenatal) disease not generally noted in past reports" (Tondury and Smith, 1966).

In some cases, youngsters who appear normal at birth may show rubella infections when serologic studies are performed (Cooper and Krugman, 1964). It is therefore imperative to continue evaluations of these children so that findings which are not immediately apparent at birth (such as central nervous system damage or hearing loss) are not overlooked and the etiology of later developing difficulties is clarified. "Prospective studies . . . have shown that some defects resulting from maternal rubella during the first trimester become apparent only as the child develops" (Weinberger *et al.*, 1970).

BEHAVIORAL STUDIES

Although an extensive body of literature exists on the physical sequelae of congenital rubella, reports on the behavioral consequences of the disease are much less common.

The results of studies conducted before the 1964 epidemic generally fall into two categories. Some investigators found no psychological patterns to distinguish rubella children from non-rubella youngsters. Others noted specific behavioral sequelae in children who contracted rubella *in utero*.

In the first group, Kirman (1955) reported on mentally defective children whose deficiency was thought to be due to maternal rubella. He reviewed records of seven children during the six years they had been hospitalized and found that "apart from the intellectual limitations there are no special psychological features common to this group."

Similarly, Bindon (1957), who administered intelligence, Rorschach, and fantasy-production tests to rubella deaf, non-rubella deaf, and normal children, found that "the rubella deaf perform no differently from non-rubella deaf children." However, as a result of their retarded language development, both deaf groups functioned at a less mature level than the hearing youngsters, even though the author could find no specific personality patterns to differentiate the subsamples.

Another investigator who found little evidence to support the theory that "rubella children often show emotional instability and difficult behavior" was Sheridan (1964). The sample he studied in this follow-up inquiry was a group of 227 youngsters aged eight to eleven years. Fifteen per cent of them had major abnormalities and a further 16% had minor defects. A total of 29% had some significant degree of hearing loss, and in 17 of these children deafness was first diagnosed at this time.

Although specific behavioral information was requested for each child, the records noted only that 12 were " 'shy,' 'immature,' 'lacking in concentration,' or 'liable to outburst of temper.' " Furthermore, "only one, a blind child, was reported as 'psychologically difficult.' " The IQ test scores of 191 children in this group showed a normal distribution, with a range of 63 to 160, and Sheridan concluded that "this inquiry has produced no evidence that mental subnormality is a common sequel of early maternal rubella."

Finally, no discussion of the positive prognostic reports on the behavior of rubella children would be complete without mention of the 25-year follow-up of Gregg's original patients (Menser *et al.*, 1967). The authors of this study were struck by the "good socioeconomic adjustment made by most patients" and concluded that "the developmental potential of many . . . had been assessed erroneously during the preschool period." It should be noted, however, that no organized developmental assessment of these patients as children is reported.

Of the early studies in which distinct behavioral sequelae of rubella were found, one of the first was done by Levine (1951). She investigated, over a period of two years, 16 children at the Lexington School for the Deaf whose mothers had had rubella during pregnancy and all but three of whom had one or more physical defects besides deafness. Thirteen of these three- to four-year-olds were "quite like other small deaf children in their general behavior and responsiveness to play and to people" except that they showed "a greater tendency to hyperactivity, tenseness and low stimulus threshold. . . . No evidence of emotional disturbance could be found to account for this." The other three children were "highly atypical in all their observed reactions. Their behavioral pictures appeared to combine infantile characteristics, defective mentality, inappropriate emotional responsiveness and queer motor mannerisms." Their general behavior was "strongly suggestive of some type of brain damage or disease."

In a study of 57 youngsters aged three to five years, Jackson and Fisch (1958) found that the "children with the most severe degree of bilateral deafness showed an abnormal behavior pattern," including restlessness, destructiveness, spitefulness, and inability to concentrate. They suggested that "more detailed behavior and intelligence studies would be necessary to determine the cause of this behavior and its relation to deafness or to brain damage unassociated with deafness," but this does not appear to have been done.

Following the 1951 epidemic of rubella in Sweden, Lundstrom and his associates began a longitudinal study of children born with the disease. One of their aims was a systematic controlled investigation of the mental development of children of school age with a history of maternal rubella (Lundstrom and Ahnsjo, 1962). They compared a group of rubella children with controls using information on the youngsters' performances on school maturity tests and answers by teachers to questionnaires to determine the psycho-educational progress of both groups. Of the 449 rubella and 403 normal children who had taken the Swedish school maturity tests, a significantly higher percentage of youngsters whose mothers had rubella during the second month of pregnancy (26%) were found to be unready for school than the controls and other rubella subgroups (7 to 17%). They also found a highly significant difference in the incidence of school entry postponement, due mainly to "lack of school maturity," between children whose mothers had rubella during the second and third months of pregnancy (13% and 11% respectively) and the controls (3%). Finally, of those who started school at the usual age, a larger percentage (30%) of children whose mothers had rubella during the second month of pregnancy were assigned to the bottom third of their classes than the controls (21%), again a significant difference.

Among the studies initiated after clinical descriptions of the expanded rubella syndrome were first presented is that of Desmond and her colleagues at Baylor University who have been following children born during the 1964 epidemic (Desmond *et al.*, 1967; 1970). Eighty-one of their original 100 patients who were seen monthly or more often until three months of age and then at three month intervals, showed neurological abnormalities of varying degree between birth and one year. At 18 months of age, 44 of the 64 survivors continued to show neurological residua including "a wide range of motor deficits, hyperactivity, restlessness, convulsions, stereotyped movements and poor progress in adaptive behavior" (Desmond *et al.*, 1970). Furthermore, the median levels of motor development, language development, adaptive behavior, and personal-social behavior for the group were all below average at 18 months. Infants with multiple handicaps had the lowest scores.

Desmond and her co-workers (1970) also reported that at 18 months of age, "eight infants appeared autistic, isolated and out of communication with the environment" and "eleven had made virtually no progress in adaptive behavior over the prior six-month period."

Freedman and his colleagues (1970) offer a description of the development of one multihandicapped rubella baby during his first eighteen months of life. They conclude that the child "fulfills most of the behavioral criteria Rimland lists as 'necessary but not sufficient' for the diagnosis of infantile autism. . . . Organismic and environmental factors operated in concert to produce atypical and maladaptive patterns of concrete experience." The authors concentrate on a strictly psychoanalytic interpretation of the child's behavior and although they state that the child's organismic handicaps are directly responsible for militating against the development of a more typical interchange between him and his environment, the relevance of their analysis to the development of other handicapped rubella children remains to be established.

Hicks (1970) studied the performance of a group of rubella deaf children on the Goodenough-Harris Draw-A-Person Test and on individually administered intelligence tests. He found no significant differences between their scores and the scores of a control group of non-rubella deaf youngsters. However, on the basis of work with the children over a two-year period, their teachers concluded that 1) "the post-rubella deaf child requires more freedom and motility within the classroom situation than do other deaf children. Though the term 'hyperactive' is probably inappropriate as a general descriptive term for their behavior there is a tendency for them to be quite active," and 2) "there is a strong tendency toward distractibility in these children. When formal lessons are attempted there appears a need for greater structure than with the non-rubella deaf child."

In any discussion of recent studies of rubella children, the work of McCay Vernon (1967; 1969) must be mentioned. In his study, in which he performed an overall evaluation of more than 1400 children at the California School for the Deaf, Vernon found that the average intelligence of the rubella deaf was significantly below that of normal children, with eight per cent retarded (IQ below 70), while their academic achievement and communication skills (measured via written language) were significantly below that of other deaf youngsters. However, it was "in terms of emotional adjustment that the rubella children (whose mean age was 15 years 6 months) were the most different from the other deaf youth." Of the 103 children whose deafness was attributed to congenital rubella, 28 were "emotionally disturbed," as measured by formal psychological evaluation. Eight of this group were called psychotic. "The rubella-affected children were often characterized by a single basic syndrome which involved extensive hyperactivity, distractibility and difficulty in remembering, sometimes accompanied by explosiveness and uncontrolled emotionality." Vernon suggests that many of these problems "have their basis in central nervous system dysfunction that is additional to the auditory impairment."

This conclusion is in line with the general proposal of Graham and Rutter (1968) following their study of school-age children on the Isle of Wight. They suggested that "the presence of a chronic physical handicap per se was not a crucial factor" in the development of childhood psychiatric disorders, nor was the severity of the handicap nor its visibility the determining influence. Rather, "the presence of dysfunction specifically of the brain was the crucial factor in the development of psychiatric disorder."

It is important to keep these statements in mind in reviewing the behavior of rubella children. Just as Wright (1971) has speculated that "mental retardation occurs in infants suffering from the rubella syndrome when rubella virus infects cells of the brain, causing cell death and slow cell growth (failure of mitosis), which ultimately results in a small organ (brain) incapable of functioning optimally," perhaps the varying behavioral characteristics found in rubella children by the investigators discussed above are ultimately to be explained by the presence or absence of central nervous system damage in a particular child. Knowledge of the action of rubella virus and the behavioral sequelae make such a conclusion almost inescapable.

2

Study Sample

FOLLOWING THE 1964 rubella epidemic, a Rubella Birth Defect Evaluation Project (RBDEP) was established at New York University Medical Center (Cooper *et al.,* 1969) to service infants whose mothers had the disease during pregnancy. In cooperation with this project, we undertook in 1967 a behavioral study to determine the psychological and psychiatric consequences of congenital rubella. Our sample consisted of 243 children enrolled with RBDEP. All of these youngsters had a diagnosis of congenital rubella confirmed by either virus isolation or serologic procedures.

Demographic Data

Demographic information on the families participating in this study was initially gathered from the records of the Rubella Birth

11

TABLE 1

ETHNIC COMPOSITION OF PARENTS

Group	Father N	%	Mother N	%
Negro	36	14.8	37	15.2
Puerto Rican	43	17.7	46	18.9
White (non-Puerto Rican)	154	63.4	151	62.2
Other	8	3.3	7	2.9
Not known	2	.8	2	.8
Total	243	100.0	243	100.0

Defect Evaluation Project. These data were revised and updated when the children were seen for testing and interviews.

The majority of the families were white (see Table 1), with an unusually high proportion of Puerto Rican families (17.7% as compared to New York City Department of Health statistics listing Puerto Ricans as comprising 7.9% of the total population). This disproportion may be due to two factors: 1) the relatively large number of Puerto Rican children in the age group considered at risk for rubella (one in three Puerto Rican children are under 14 years of age, whereas one in five non-Puerto Rican white children are under 14); 2) the lower median incomes of these families and the greater probability of overcrowded living conditions, thus increasing the likelihood that pregnant Puerto Rican women were more exposed to rubella during the 1964 epidemic than their representation in the population would by itself indicate.

The religious affiliations of the families are detailed in Table 2.

The socioeconomic status of the families participating in the behavioral study was widely distributed. Although the vast majority of the mothers were housewives, the fathers' occupations ranged from unskilled and semiskilled labor to the professions. The details are given in Table 3.

TABLE 2

RELIGIOUS AFFILIATION OF PARENTS

Religion	Father N	%	Mother N	%
Catholic	135	55.5	139	57.2
Protestant	42	17.3	40	16.5
Jewish	29	11.9	30	12.3
Other	6	2.5	7	2.9
Not Known	31	12.8	27	11.1
Total	243	100.0	243	100.0

TABLE 3

OCCUPATION OF PARENTS

Occupation	Fathers N	%	Mothers N	%
Unemployed	9	3.7	—	—
Housewife	—	—	188	77.4
Unskilled & Semiskilled	53	21.8	18	7.4
Skilled	85	35.0	4	1.6
Clerical and Sales	46	18.9	9	3.7
Student	1	0.4	—	—
Professional	43	17.7	16	6.6
Not Known	6	2.5	8	3.3
Total	243	100.0	243	100.0

Physical Status of the Children

Of the 243 children in the behavioral study, 124 were boys and 119 were girls. They ranged in age from 2½ to 4 years when they were first seen by us. The majority of the children (178 or 73.3%) had been infected with rubella while their mothers were in the first trimester of pregnancy; 30 children (12.3%) were infected during the mother's second trimester of pregnancy; and 4 (1.6%) were infected during her third trimester. In 31 cases

TABLE 4

KNOWN BIRTHWEIGHTS OF CHILDREN IN THE BEHAVIORAL STUDY

Weight (in ounces)	N	%
Under 80	57	23.5
80-88	40	16.5
89-96	26	10.7
97-104	27	11.1
105-112	26	10.7
113-120	19	7.8
121-128	7	2.9
129-136	10	4.1
137-144	3	11.5
Total	215	98.8

(12.8%) the gestational age at which rubella occurred was not known.

From the records of the RBDEP we were able to determine the birthweights of most of the children. These are shown in Table 4.

One is immediately struck by the large number of children (40%) whose birthweight was less than 88 ounces (5 pounds 8 ounces) and who can thus be described as premature. This figure far exceeds those given in most discussions of the incidence of prematurity. Of the total number of children born in the United States in 1965, only 8.3% had birthweights under 2500 grams (88 ounces). It should also be noted that whereas 7.2% of all white (including Puerto Rican) babies weighed less than 2500 grams at birth, double this amount, or 13.8%, of nonwhite infants were premature by weight (National Center for Health Statistics, 1965). In our sample, therefore, the incidence of prematurity was five times greater than that found in the general population of children and three times that of the nonwhite population. This is in accord with the figures of other authors who have found approximately half or more of the rubella children they studied to be premature (Lindquist *et al.,* 1965; Michaels and Kenny, 1969; Monif *et al.,* 1966).

Our data on the physical status of the rubella children were taken from the records of the RBDEP. Their staff reviewed the findings at intervals determined by "clinical need or a regular schedule (e.g., pediatric examination annually), whichever was more frequent" (Cooper *et al.,* 1969). We tabulated the physical data on each child at the point in time closest to our first direct contact with him. This decision was necessitated by the fact that the children we studied did not have a fixed pathology during their young lives. In some cases, as a result of the continuing nature of the fetally-acquired rubella infection, defects became evident or more pronounced some time after birth. For example, some children developed cataracts during infancy which were not present in the immediate neonatal period. In other cases, the physical status of a child may have been altered through the application of various remedial procedures, such as cardiac surgery, cataract removal, and the use of eyeglasses and hearing aids. In still other instances, rubella-related findings at birth, such as purpura or transient bone lesions, were self limited conditions that disappeared with age.

The physical status of the children was quite varied when we first saw them. About one-fifth of the sample (50 children) were considered to have no defects, despite earlier serological evidence of rubella. Another fourth had only one area of physical defect. A summary of these findings is presented in Table 5.

Throughout the literature on rubella, certain specific physical and organic findings are consistently related to fetal infection. Some of these, since they have no functional implications, were not considered to be more than diagnostically significant by the RBDEP and therefore were not tabulated by us. In this category were such findings as tooth-enamel mottling and retinopathy, both of which may aid in the clinical diagnosis of congenital rubella but which do not interfere with functioning. We also did not tabulate conditions (purpura, bone lesions, hemolytic anemia,

TABLE 5

Physical Status of Rubella Children

Number of Defects	N	%
Well (no defect)	50	20.6
One area of defect	72	29.6
Two areas of defect	47	19.3
Three areas of defect	47	19.3
Four areas of defect	27	11.1
Total	243	99.9

etc.) which had disappeared or been corrected by the time of our study.

We categorized the rubella-related defects reported to us by the RBDEP as follows:

1. *Visual*: cataracts, glaucoma, myopia, microphthalmia, eso-tropia, nystagmus, ptosis, and strabismus. Visual defects were further broken down according to degrees of severity. Thus, unilateral or bilateral microphthalmia, esotropia, nystagmus, and ptosis were grouped as mild defects (1) ; unilateral cataract, glaucoma, and strabismus as moderate (2) ; and bilateral cataract, glaucoma, and strabismus as severe (3). Rubella retinopathy, although found in many of the children, was not included as a handicap, since it is a non-interfering defect.

2. *Hearing*: losses of unspecified (1), moderate (2), or severe or profound (3) degree.

3. *Neurological*: hard signs, as spasticity, cerebral palsy, seizures, paresis, or encephalitis; and soft signs, as myotonia, clumsiness of gait, and falling. (We did not include neuromotor retardation in our classification of neurological defect because it is identical with the psychiatric diagnosis of mental retardation.)

4. *Cardiac*: unspecified congenital heart disease, patent ductus arteriosis, pulmonic stenosis, aortic stenosis, atrial septal defect, and ventricular defect.

TABLE 6

CHILDREN WITH SPECIFIC PHYSICAL DEFECTS

Specific Defect	Number of Children
Visual	80 (32.9%)
Hearing	177 (72.8%)
Neurological	79 (32.5%)
Cardiac	79 (32.5%)

TABLE 7

PHYSICAL DEFECT COMBINATIONS

Single Defect:	Number of Children
Hearing	65
Visual	4
Cardiac	2
Neurological	1
Total Single	72

Double Defect:	
Hearing & Neurological	18
Hearing & Visual	14
Hearing and Cardiac	10
Visual & Neurological	1
Neurological & Cardiac	2
Visual & Cardiac	2
Total Double	47

Triple Defect:	
Hearing, Visual & Cardiac	17
Hearing, Cardiac & Neurological	15
Hearing, Visual & Neurological	11
Visual, Cardiac & Neurological	4
Total Triple	47

Total Quadruple:	
Hearing, Visual, Cardiac & Neurological	27

An analysis of the incidence of specific defects highlights the fact that the most common sequela of congenital rubella is some degree of hearing loss, either by itself or in combination with other handicaps. Table 6 lists the number of children with hearing, visual, neurologic, and cardiac defects. The total is greater than 243 as many children had more than one defect.

Every child was also classified in terms of the kind and severity of his defect as they were found in combination. For example, a child might be listed as Visual 1, Hearing 3, Neurological. This indicates that he had a mild visual defect, severe hearing loss, and neurological signs. A detailed listing of the physical defect combinations found in this sample is given in Table 7, and Table 8 shows the defect combinations according to severity.

Consideration of the incidence of specific defects in this group of children and comparisons with other samples reported in the literature are beyond the scope of this monograph for two main reasons. First, we cannot judge how representative our sample of children was of the total population of youngsters with congenital

TABLE 8

SUMMARY OF PHYSICAL DEFECT COMBINATIONS, INCLUDING DEGREE OF SEVERITY

Note: Hearing and visual defects are graded by their severity, 1 being the mildest deficit and 3 the greatest. The specific criteria for each diagnosis are given in the text.

Single Defect:	N
Visual—2	2
Visual—3	2
Hearing—1	4
Hearing—2	14
Hearing—3	47
Neurological	1
Cardiac	2
Total Single Defect	72

Double Defect:

Visual—1 & Neurological	1
Visual—2 & Cardiac	1
Visual—3 & Cardiac	1
Hearing—1 & Cardiac	1
Hearing—1 & Neurological	1
Hearing—1 & Visual—2	1
Hearing—1 & Visual—3	2
Hearing—2 & Neurological	4
Hearing—2 & Cardiac	5
Hearing—2 & Visual—1	1
Hearing—2 & Visual—2	3
Hearing—3 & Neurological	13
Hearing—3 & Cardiac	4
Hearing—3 & Visual—1	2
Hearing—3 & Visual—2	4
Hearing—3 & Visual—3	1
Neurological & Cardiac	2
	—
Total Double Defect	47

Triple Defect:

Visual—2 & Cardiac & Neurological	1
Visual—3 & Cardiac & Neurological	3
Hearing—1 & Cardiac & Neurological	2
Hearing—1 & Visual—1 & Neurological	1
Hearing—1 & Visual—2 & Cardiac	2
Hearing—2 & Cardiac & Neurological	2
Hearing—2 & Visual—2 & Cardiac	2
Hearing—2 & Visual—3 & Neurological	1
Hearing—3 & Cardiac & Neurological	11
Hearing—3 & Visual—1 & Neurological	1
Hearing—3 & Visual—2 & Cardiac	9
Hearing—3 & Visual—2 & Neurological	5
Hearing—3 & Visual—3 & Cardiac	4
Hearing—3 & Visual—3 & Neurological	3
	—
Total Triple Defect	47

Quadruple Defect:

Hearing—1 & Visual—1 & Neurological & Cardiac	1
Hearing—1 & Visual—2 & Neurological & Cardiac	1
Hearing—1 & Visual—3 & Neurological & Cardiac	5
Hearing—2 & Visual—2 & Neurological & Cardiac	4
Hearing—2 & Visual—3 & Neurological & Cardiac	2
Hearing—3 & Visual—1 & Neurological & Cardiac	1
Hearing—3 & Visual—2 & Neurological & Cardiac	7
Hearing—3 & Visual—3 & Neurological & Cardiac	6
	—
Total Quadruple Defect	27

TABLE 9

DEFECT COMBINATIONS MOST FREQUENTLY FOUND

Physical Status	Number of Children
No Defect	50
Hearing Severe	47
Hearing Moderate	14
Hearing Severe & Neurological	13
Hearing Severe & Neurological & Cardiac	11
Hearing Severe & Visual Moderate & Cardiac	9
Hearing Severe & Visual Moderate & Cardiac & Neurological	7
Hearing Severe & Visual Severe & Cardiac & Neurological	6
Total	157

rubella following the 1964 epidemic. Secondly, the focus of this study was on behavioral consequences of the disease and we did not ourselves investigate physical sequelae beyond their possible effect on psychological functioning.

It is interesting to note, however, the extremely varied sequelae of congenital rubella. This is indicated by both the number of groups needed to categorize all the children and the fact that only eight of these groups (including those with no defects) contained six or more children. These eight groups are listed in Table 9, and 157 of the 243 children fit into them.

The largest single group, excluding the 50 youngsters apparently unaffected, consists of 47 children with severe hearing loss. Next in size is the group of 14 children with moderate hearing impairment. Severe hearing loss in combination with clinically identifiable neurological findings follows with 13 children. Eleven youngsters with severe hearing impairment had both neurological and cardiac findings. Another 9 youngsters were simultaneously afflicted with severe hearing loss, moderate visual impairment, and cardiac defects, and an additional 7 had these same findings plus neurological defects. The final group of 6 had severe hearing loss, severe visual loss, neurological findings, and congenital cardiac defects. The remaining 86 children in our study sample were spread among 39 defect groups. In 16 of these, the particular combination of defect and severity was unique to an individual child.

It is important to look at our children in this manner because every combination of handicap resulted in some special consequences with regard to their functioning.

For example, two children with moderate hearing losses and cataract in one eye were both aided through the use of hearing aids and cataract removal. Yet one also had spastic diplegia, for which he wore leg braces, and was of average intelligence, while the other had no motor neurological pathology but was moderately retarded. The two children's adaptive capacities and their needs for appropriate management and proper educational placement were completely different.

Thus, each subgroup, even if represented by a single child, must be taken into account. Each subgroup, though it may not in itself be statistically significant, indicates a child with real problems who has specific needs for remediation and special social and educational management.

Family Data

In order to facilitate studies of family relationships and parental attitudes, it was necessary to determine the ordinal position of each child and the number of his siblings. These factors can be of great value in surveying a child's familial environment. The largest percentage of the children (39.1%) were first born, and most of them had at least one brother or sister. Details are given in Table 10.

Since our aim was to assess the behavioral functioning of these rubella children, we had to have psychiatric, psychologic, and social evaluations. We obtained this information through direct evaluation and testing of the youngsters and an interview with their parents. Although we attempted to get as complete a picture as possible of every child, we were not always successful in having each youngster and his parents seen by the psychiatrist, psycholo-

TABLE 10

ORDINAL POSITION & NUMBER OF CHILDREN IN FAMILY

Ordinal Position	N	%
First Born	95	39.1
Second Born	46	18.9
Third Born	54	22.2
Fourth Born	15	6.2
Fifth Born	15	6.2
Sixth Born	6	2.5
Seventh Born	4	1.6
Eighth Born	3	1.2
Twin (one of)	8	3.3
Not Known	5	2.1
Total*	251	103.3

* Adds up to more than 243 as twins are listed both separately and according to ordinal position.

Number of Children in Family	N	%
One	33	13.6
Two	74	30.4
Three	64	26.3
Four	31	12.8
Five	20	8.2
Six	7	2.9
Seven	5	2.1
Eight	1	0.4
Nine	3	1.2
Not Known	5	2.1
Total	243	100.0

gist, and social worker. In a number of cases, this was because the child had been institutionalized. Nevertheless, every one of the 243 children in the sample was seen by at least one of the professionals on our staff or the staff of the institution at which he was an inpatient.

OTHER SAMPLES USED FOR COMPARISON

In order to place our findings on the behavioral characteristics of rubella children in proper perspective, we found it useful to compare them with data obtained in two other studies in which one of us (S.C.) was the chief investigator. These were studies of the behavioral characteristics of intellectually normal and of mentally retarded children. A brief description of the samples of children in these studies is given here as a guide for later discussions.

New York Longitudinal Study (NYLS): The children in this study were of relatively homogeneous middle- or upper-middle-class families living in New York City or its suburbs. The youngsters were enrolled at birth and a total of 136 children from 85 families have been studied for the past fifteen years. We have nese and one Negro family are enrolled. Forty percent of the with the rubella children to insure age-equivalence.

The study families are predominantly Jewish (78%) with some Catholic (7%) and Protestant (15%) families. One Chiused only data obtained in the preschool period for comparisons mothers and 60% of the fathers had both college education and postgraduate degrees. All but three of the fathers worked either in one of the professions or in business at an executive or management level. Eighty percent of the mothers had occupations similar to the fathers, and the remaining 20% had been employed as secretaries or office workers.

Data on the NYLS youngsters were gathered through 1) detailed behavioral histories obtained from the parents at three-month intervals during the child's first year and then at six-month intervals; 2) periods of direct observation during infancy; 3) direct observation of the child's behavior during a standard play and psychological test situation at three years of age; 4) direct observation of the child's behavior in nursery school; and 5) teacher interviews.

Psychiatric evaluations were arranged when the parents requested them because of troublesome behavior in the child. In 17 cases a psychiatric diagnosis was made by age five. One child had a severe behavior disorder secondary to brain damage and the remainder had reactive behavior disorders of a degree varying from mild to moderately severe (Thomas *et al.,* 1963; Thomas *et al.,* 1968).

Mentally Retarded Study: The sample in this study was a relatively homogeneous group of 52 children between the ages of 5 years and 11 years 11 months. All were from middle-class families and lived at home; none had ever been institutionalized. Their retardation had been identified at an early age and all the youngsters attended special classes in public or private schools. The parents' educational level ranged from high school to post-graduate work.

The mental ages of these children ranged from 4 to 6 years and their IQs were from 50 to 75.

Although 24 of the children had soft neurological signs, such as poor coordination, poor muscle tone, or hyperreflexia, any youngster who had motor dysfunction of a degree that would interfere significantly with his level of functioning in everyday life was systematically excluded from the study.

Data on the retarded children were collected in a manner similar to that used in the NYLS. There were interviews with parents and teachers and direct observations of each child at home and in school. In addition, each child was given a psychological test, a clinical psychiatric evaluation, and a neurological examination. Thirty-one of the 52 children studied (60%) were judged to have a psychiatric disorder (Chess and Hassibi, 1970; Chess and Korn, 1970).

3

Prevalence of Psychiatric Casualty

DIAGNOSING AND TABULATING the psychiatric problems found in rubella children is not merely an exercise in classification. Rather, as with any diagnosis, the purpose in defining the problem is to facilitate remediation and therapy. By identifying the developmental and behavioral consequences of rubella in the preschool period, we can prepare to meet the special needs of these youngsters at the earliest possible time.

It has been estimated that at least 20,000 children in the United States were born damaged as a result of the 1964 rubella epidemic. An examination of the behavioral problems in even a small part of this group, the 243 youngsters we studied, may suggest the kind of effort required to establish appropriate services for these children.

Furthermore, although we can point to a specific virus as the cause of the defects in our sample, the number and combination of the rubella children's physical and intellectual defects resemble those found in other groups of multihandicapped children with varying etiologies (genetic factors, intrauterine insults, prematurity, anoxia at birth, postnatal insult or injury). Many of our findings will, therefore, be applicable to this even larger population of youngsters who are likely to have similar special needs.

PSYCHIATRIC STUDY

The first issue to be considered was how many of the rubella children showed behavioral deviations, and in what diagnostic categories and how frequently these disorders occurred.

Psychiatric diagnoses were made on the basis of 1) direct examination of the children, usually in a specially-equipped playroom (although some were seen at home or at Willowbrook State School) ; 2) historical behavioral descriptions of the children obtained from the parents; and 3) descriptions of the children's behavior obtained from their nursery school teachers or the staff of the RBDEP. In 171 cases, the diagnoses were based primarily on structured psychiatric and psychological examinations. In 63 cases, the diagnoses were based primarily on descriptive reports of the children's behavior at home as it was observed and recorded by a member of the study team. And in 9 cases not seen by any member of our study team, those children who were institutionalized, the diagnoses of the Willowbrook staff were accepted as valid. In all instances, supplementary information culled from the available behavioral descriptions was taken into account in making a diagnosis. All diagnoses were reviewed by one of the authors (S.C.) .

An attempt was made to see each child alone during the formal psychiatric examination. However, if it appeared that separation anxiety or physical frailty would interfere with observation of a significant range of the youngster's behavioral capacities, one or both parents were invited into the playroom. After the child had some time to become relaxed with the examiner, he was offered a variety of toys suitable for preschool children that presented possibilities of both quiet and active play. Included were blocks, doll house furniture, family dolls, hand puppets, trucks, puzzles, paper, pencils, crayons, blackboard and chalk, darts and targets, etc. The examiner recorded the level, content, and characteristics of the child's play, verbalizations, and affective relatedness. Any symptoms demonstrated during this session were noted.

The examiner also had a brief conference with the parents during which they were asked to state what, if any, aspects of the child's behavior were troublesome to them and what measures they used to cope with these. Where appropriate, the child's problems were immediately discussed with the parents, who received recommendations as to intervention.

CATEGORIES OF PSYCHIATRIC DIAGNOSIS

Diagnoses were made in accordance with the classification system reported by one of us (Chess, 1969). We considered the following possible diagnostic categories: normal, cerebral dysfunction, reactive behavior disorder, neurotic behavior disorder, neurotic character disorder, neurosis, childhood psychosis and schizophrenic adjustments, sociopathic personality, and mental retardation.

The number of children found in each psychiatric category is presented in Table 11. It should be noted that if a child had more than one psychiatric disorder he was tabulated in each category separately. For example, a child with both mental retardation and a reactive behavior disorder is listed in each group.

No Psychiatric Disorder

Normalcy is more than the absence of pathology. A normal child shows a developmental level in accord with established norms, gets along reasonably well with his parents, siblings, and

TABLE 11

PSYCHIATRIC DIAGNOSES OF 243 CHILDREN

No Psychiatric Disorder (Normal)	118
Cerebral Dysfunction	8
Reactive Behavior Disorder	37
Autism	10
Partial Syndrome of Autism	8
Mental Retardation—unspecified	7
Mental Retardation—borderline	11
Mental Retardation—mild	10
Mental Retardation—moderate	20
Mental Retardation—severe	31
Mental Retardation—profound	12
Total*	272

* Adds up to more than 243 as several children fit into more than one category.

friends, and has no significant manifestations of behavioral disturbance. He uses his apparent intellectual potential to a degree close to his capacity and is contented for a reasonable portion of his waking hours.

Approximately half of our rubella children showed no behavioral pathology. However, looked at from the point of view of a youngster's risk of psychiatric disorder, if we can generalize from this sample, a child whose mother had rubella during pregnancy has a fifty per cent chance of having some type of behavioral disturbance.

Cerebral Dysfunction

This diagnosis is made only in those cases in which independent evidence of neurological disease of the brain coexists with a behavior disorder characterized by symptoms generally associated with brain damage. Hypo- or hyperactivity, attention abnormalities, and impulse disorders are some of the symptoms that might alert one to this diagnosis, but it can only be made if neurological signs are also present. Similarly, a child who is neurologically shown to have brain damage would not be given a psychiatric diagnosis of cerebral dysfunction unless he also shows specific behavioral pathology. Certain maturational lags may properly be included here if they are found in association with demonstrable brain damage. By convention, mental retardation is classified separately though it may be found in association with cerebral dysfunction.

If the diagnosis of cerebral dysfunction were based solely on the presence of chronic brain infection, it could probably be used to describe the great majority of children with congenital rubella. Reports from a number of centers, especially those of Desmond and her colleagues at Baylor University (1967; 1970), have documented the fact that elevated protein levels, pleocytosis, and the rubella virus itself are frequently found in the cerebrospinal fluid of the survivors of prenatal infections. Furthermore, autopsy studies have demonstrated widespread destructive vascular and parenchymal lesions in children who had congenital rubella.

Using our rigorous criteria, which require the presence of both neurological and behavioral pathology, only eight children warranted the specific diagnosis of cerebral dysfunction. Two of these youngsters were intellectually normal and six showed varying degrees of retardation. These eight children represent 3.3 per cent of our study population. By contrast, only one child in the New York Longitudinal Study was diagnosed as having cerebral dysfunction by the age of five. (The other two brain-damaged children did not have any behavior disorders by this age.) In the mentally retarded study, however, 21.2 per cent of the children were given a diagnosis of cerebral dysfunction. The high incidence of such disorders in these chronologically older children is of interest in terms of predicting what may happen to the rubella children. It is probable that more of them will be found at a later age to show behavioral pathology. This prognosis is warranted by the fact that behavioral limitations and aberrations may well become evident later in life when the rubella children are faced with increased demands for impulse control and flexibility of functioning not now made of them in their preschool years.

Reactive Behavior Disorder

When external circumstances and environmental handling are inappropriate for a particular child, stress may develop. The child's aberrant functioning as a result of this stress may be diagnosed as a reactive behavior disorder. The term "reactive" implies that with a beneficial change in the circumstances producing the disorder there will be a corresponding improvement in the child's behavior. A typical history might include difficulty at home but no problems in school or *vice versa*.

Thirty-seven children (15 per cent of the total sample) had reactive behavior disorders. By comparison, 11 per cent of the NYLS were given this diagnosis by the age of five while 34.6 per cent of the Mentally Retarded sample were also so diagnosed. Thus, the incidence of reactive behavior disorders was only slightly increased in the rubella children over the normal children. However, in view of the very high incidence of this disturbance in the retardates, this trend may reflect the excessive stress imposed on handicapped youngsters in their daily lives as they grow older.

Childhood Psychosis and Schizophrenic Adjustments—
Autism and Partial Syndrome of Autism

Psychosis is diagnosed when a child's behavior is disorganized and out of touch with reality. The diagnosis of schizophrenic adjustment implies the presence of deviations in thought processes, affect, interpersonal relatedness, motility, and speech patterns which are just short of an actual psychotic state.

In our study, we considered autism in the category of childhood psychosis and schizophrenic adjustments. The primary criteria for this diagnosis are indications that the child has an affective defect and makes frantic attempts to maintain the sameness of environmental details. Possible symptoms as reported originally by Kanner (1943) include: 1) Inability to relate in the ordinary way to people and situations from the beginning of life; 2) Monotonously repetitive verbal utterances which do not convey meaning to others. Delayed echolalia; 3) Excellent rote memory but inability to use language in any other way; 4) Viewing as a dreaded intrusion everything impinging on the child from the outside (including food, noise, motion) ; 5) Limited spontaneous activity; and 6) Good relation to objects, with which the child can play happily for hours.

None of the rubella children gave evidence of a psychosis or childhood schizophrenia other than autism. Ten youngsters were diagnosed as autistic, and their behavior corresponded to Kanner's criteria except for the additional finding of mental retardation in all but one of them. Furthermore, another eight children showed a significant number of signs of autistic behavior, though their total behavioral picture failed to correspond rigorously to Kanner's criteria for early infantile autism. In these cases, the term "partial syndrome of autism" was employed.

The extremely high prevalence of autism in this sample is underlined when our figures are compared with those found in studies of the general child population. A survey of British children in Middlesex aged from eight to ten years done in 1964 found 2.1 per 10,000 to have behavior "closest to that of Kanner's syndrome," while another 2.4 per 10,000 showed autistic behavior but with less motor abnormality (Lotter, 1966) .

In a survey of Wisconsin children by Treffert (1970) , classical infantile autism was found in 0.7 per 10,000 youngsters, while the total childhood schizophrenia group, including autism, had a prevalence rate of 3.1 per 10,000. In striking contrast, the prevalence rate in our rubella children would correspond to 412 per 10,000 for the core syndrome of autism and 329 per 10,000 for the partial syndrome, yielding a combined figure of 741 per 10,000! The implications of this high prevalence are discussed in Chapter 9.

Mental Retardation

The psychiatric diagnosis of mental retardation refers to "subnormal general intellectual functioning which originates during the developmental period and is associated with impairment of either learning and social adjustment or maturation or both" (APA, 1968).

The children who were mentally retarded comprised the largest deviant subsample of the group we studied. Ninety-one youngsters, 37% of the total sample, were retarded. Since most surveys indicate that in any population of children 2% to 3% are likely to be retarded, the excessive incidence here may be considered a direct consequence of fetal rubella.

We further classified the mentally retarded children in accordance with standard subdivisions indicating degree of subnormality: borderline, mild, moderate, severe, profound, and unspecified. In general surveys, it has been found that the vast majority of retarded youngsters fall into the borderline or mild groups. As the degree of retardation becomes more severe, the number of children in each category usually drops sharply. In this study, the reverse trend was apparent. Those children who were severely retarded comprised the largest group, and the combination of those who were severely or profoundly retarded represented almost half of the total group of retardates (43 of 91). Thus, congenital rubella appears not only to make a child vulnerable to retardation but also to put him at risk of having a moderate to profound deficit.

OTHER DIAGNOSTIC CATEGORIES

Although all the children we studied fell into one or more of the psychiatric categories discussed above, mention should be made of the other classifications available, since they may pertain to the rubella youngsters when they are followed up at a later age. These diagnoses would not be found among preschool children primarily because their personalities and developmental levels are not yet capable of such complex reactive patterns.

Neurotic Behavior Disorder

When behavioral difficulties of a reactive type become fixated patterns that manifest themselves even in favorable situations and after the stress has been relieved, the term neurotic becomes appropriate. The behavior patterns in this category differ from reactive behavior disorders not only in terms of the rigidity with which they are established but also in that they may be the beginning of compulsions, phobias, or hysterical reactions which, with further fixation and organization, may develop into obsessive-compulsive or other neuroses.

Neurotic Character Disorder

This classification represents a further progression and fixation of a neurotic behavior disorder. The diagnosis is warranted when the inappropriate behaviors can be considered part of the personality organization rather than a pathological imposition. While the untoward behavior patterns may have a clear relationship to continuing inappropriate environmental stimuli, there is a marked rigidity and fixation of behavior.

Neurosis

This category corresponds in every respect to the definition of neurosis in the *Diagnostic and Statistical Manual II* of the American Psychiatric Association (1968). Obsessions, compulsions, and somatizations are commonly found mechanisms by which anxiety is avoided or represented only in disguised or symbolic form. Insofar as a child makes such adaptations to difficult situations, he can avoid the circumstances that create anxiety. In this way, the specific neurosis enables him partially to deny the reality of his personal difficulties.

Sociopathic Personality

This diagnosis has replaced the older term "psychopathic personality." An individual in this category, while apparently able to function in superficial relationships and short-term endeavors, cannot make meaningful deep relationships or defer immediate desires in order to make long-term commitments or future plans. In addition, he does not feel guilt or anxiety over injuring others and has poor impulse control and a poor sense of personal responsibility. This diagnosis is rare in young children, as the behaviors of an adult sociopath in large part would not be inappropriate in a preschool youngster.

PSYCHIATRIC DIAGNOSES OF INDIVIDUAL CHILDREN

The discussion so far has dealt mainly with the incidence of specific disorders in this group of rubella children. In order to understand the children themselves more completely, however, we must also look at the combinations of psychiatric deviations as they were actually found. Just as more than one physical defect was frequently found in a youngster, multiple psychiatric diagnoses often had to be made. This highlights the devastating effects of fetal rubella, as may be seen in Table 12.

Of the 125 children with a psychiatric problem, 99 (79.2%) had a single disorder. For the most part these were children with either a reactive behavior disorder $(N = 30)$ or some degree of mental retardation $(N = 65)$.

Twenty-six youngsters had behavioral pathology ascribable to more than one diagnosis. Five children had a combination of mental retardation and reactive behavior disorders. Nine children were both mentally retarded and autistic and six others combined mental retardation with a partial syndrome of autism. The remaining six youngsters all had a core diagnosis of cerebral dysfunction plus mental retardation, but two of them had additional reactive behavior disorders and one also showed a partial syndrome of autism.

This rather formidable array of behavioral handicaps is the legacy of the rubella epidemic to this sample of children. As we discuss later, physical and behavioral normalcy tend to be found

TABLE 12

Psychiatric Diagnoses of Individual Children

	Number	%
No Psychiatric Disorder	118	48.6
Cerebral Dysfunction	2	0.8
Cerebral Dysfunction with Mental Retardation, unspecified	1	0.4
Cerebral Dysfunction with Mental Retardation, mild	1	0.4
Cerebral Dysfunction with Mental Retardation, severe	1	0.4
Cerebral Dysfunction with Mental Retardation, mild + Reactive Behavior Disorder	1	0.4
Cerebral Dysfunction with Mental Retardation, moderate + Reactive Behavior Disorder	1	0.4
Reactive Behavior Disorder	30	12.3
Autism	1	0.4
Partial Syndrome of Autism	1	0.4
Mental Retardation, unspecified	1	0.4
Mental Retardation, borderline	7	2.9
Mental Retardation, mild	7	2.9
Mental Retardation, moderate	13	5.4
Mental Retardation, severe	26	10.7
Mental Retardation, profound	11	4.5
Reactive Behavior Disorder + Mental Retardation, borderline	2	0.8
Reactive Behavior Disorder + Mental Retardation, moderate	2	0.8
Reactive Behavior Disorder + Mental Retardation, severe	1	0.4
Mental Retardation, unspecified + Autism	2	0.8
Mental Retardation, borderline + Autism	2	0.8
Mental Retardation, moderate + Autism	1	0.4
Mental Retardation, severe + Autism	3	1.2
Mental Retardation, profound + Autism	1	0.4
Mental Retardation, unspecified + Partial Syndrome of Autism	3	1.2
Mental Retardation, moderate + Partial Syndrome of Autism	3	1.2
Cerebral Dysfunction with Mental Retardation, mild + Partial Syndrome of Autism	1	0.4
Total	243	99.7

TABLE 13

PSYCHIATRIC DIAGNOSES OF MENTALLY RETARDED STUDY CHILDREN AND THE MENTALLY RETARDED RUBELLA CHILDREN

	Rubella Study		Mentally Retarded Study	
	N	%	N	%
Mental Retardation, no other behavior disorder	65	71.4	21	40.4
Mental Retardation plus Cerebral Dysfunction	3	3.3	11	21.2
Mental Retardation plus Reactive Behavior Disorder	5	5.5	18	34.6
Mental Retardation plus Reactive Behavior Disorder plus Cerebral Dysfunction	2	2.2	0	0.0
Mental Retardation plus Autism	9	9.9	0	0.0
Mental Retardation plus Partial Syndrome of Autism	6	6.6	0	0.0
Mental Retardation plus Cerebral Dysfunction plus Partial Syndrome of Autism	1	1.1	0	0.0
Mental Retardation plus Neurotic Behavior Disorder	0	0.0	1	1.9
Mental Retardation plus Psychosis	0	0.0	1	1.9
Total	91	100.0	52	100.0

together. The behavioral problems appeared largely in physically damaged children, making remedial and therapeutic planning most difficult.

PSYCHIATRIC DIAGNOSES IN THE MENTALLY RETARDED CHILDREN

Since over one-third of our sample (91 children) were mentally retarded, we decided to isolate them for closer psychiatric study. And, in order for their particular problems to be especially meaningful, we compared them with the group of 52 mentally retarded youngsters who were subjects in a separate study described in Chapter 2 (see Table 13). In this latter group of somewhat older, sensorially intact children who lived under the most favorable possible conditions, it can be assumed that the prevalence of psychiatric problems was fairly low to the extent that optimal environment played a part in inhibiting the development of behavior disorders (Chess and Korn, 1970).

While 71% of the mentally retarded rubella children showed no behavioral pathology other than could be accounted for by their lowered cognitive capacities and developmental levels, this was true of only 40% of the Mentally Retarded study children. One may conjecture that some, if not all, of this difference may be accounted for by differences in their ages. As the rubella youngsters leave the preschool period, the number who develop behavior disorders may grow because of several factors: 1) With increasing age, the children's lives will no longer easily be restricted to the familiar home environment and they can no longer comfortably be protected against traumatic and stressful events. 2) With increasing age, the children's awareness of negative social attitudes and their development of defensive counterreactions will be greater. 3) Disabilities in capacity not entirely accounted for by their mental age may become prominent as the children become older and greater expectations arise. 4) Certain behaviors, such as tantrums, are not classified as behavior disorders in the preschool period if they are few in number. However, as the children grow older, continuation of such behaviors would require their designation as behavioral symptoms since they are out of place developmentally and become major management issues by virtue of the youngster's size and strength.

About 6.6% of the mentally retarded rubella children showed behavioral symptoms of cerebral dysfunction as opposed to 21% of the Mentally Retarded study children. This difference is especially interesting in that youngsters with hard neurological signs or sensory defects were specifically excluded from the mentally retarded study. Nevertheless, the discrepancy is in the anticipated direction since, with increasing age and new demands, an increase in behavioral disabilities due to brain damage can be expected to come to light. Deficiencies in thought processes and problems in coordination may arise within the school situation. Some of these could have been present while the child was younger, but were probably viewed as temporary lags.

In looking at the incidence of cerebral dysfunction in these two groups, it should be recalled that the autistic children were considered separately, even though we believe that they, as well as those with partial syndrome of autism, probably have gross cerebral damage. If we include these youngsters, the incidence of mentally retarded children with cerebral damage in the rubella sample increases to 23.1%, practically equivalent to that found in the mentally retarded study.

The reactive behavior disorder category shows a large difference between the groups, with 7 retarded rubella youngsters (8%) and 18 Mentally Retarded study children (35%) showing this disorder. In this area, behavior disorders in the older mentally retarded children may be prognostic of the stresses that will be faced by the rubella youngsters in the years to come. Whether their additional sensory problems will cause still greater stress, or whether the clarity of their need for a special environment will allow them greater and continued protection, cannot be guessed at this time. In addition, it may be that children now diagnosed as having reactive behavior disorders may later be evaluated as showing signs of cerebral dysfunction. One youngster in our study, who was seen by our staff three years after his initial evaluation in a special consultation for the RBDEP, showed just this progression. Seeing him at school-age, it was apparent that his disordered behavior was the direct result of cerebral dysfunction, even though at the earlier age his symptoms were reactive to environmental demands.

One child in the Mentally Retarded study sample was diagnosed as having a neurotic behavior disorder. The rubella youngsters were too immature developmentally to have such organized and fixated psychological defenses.

One Mentally Retarded study child was psychotic in addition to being mentally retarded. Neither this youngster nor any other in the study was judged to be autistic or to show a partial syndrome of autism, although a number of them had repetitive motor and verbal behaviors and had incorporated cherished rituals into their daily styles (Chess and Hassibi, 1970). The nine mentally retarded rubella children with autism and the seven with partial syndrome are a phenomenon related to rubella itself. The many implications of this finding are discussed in a separate section (see Chapter 9).

4

Physical Impairment and
Psychiatric Status

UP TO NOW WE HAVE considered physical and psychiatric data separately and described the children as fitting into normal or deviant groups within each category alone. But the children's physical condition and psychiatric status were inextricably implicated in their total adaptation. To see these youngsters as they actually functioned, we must view them simultaneously from both perspectives.

The high incidence of psychiatric disorders in the rubella children raised several questions about the correlation between physical and behavioral impairment. How were the psychiatric diagnoses related to the number of physical defects, the specific area of defect, the various combinations of defect? Such correlations can be useful in identifying children who are most at risk

40

for psychiatric disorder. In addition, these correlations may be helpful in elucidating the role of organic and environmental factors in the etiology of behavior disorders.

DEFECT AREAS AND THE PSYCHIATRIC DIAGNOSES

In Table 14 we have tabulated the children in terms of their psychiatric diagnoses and the number of areas in which they had physical defects.

It is not surprising that of the 118 children with no psychiatric disorders, 40 had no physical defects at all and 41 had only one area of physical damage. As the number of areas in which defects were present increases, the number of children without psychiatric disorders decreases. In the group of youngsters who were free of behavioral pathology there were 24 with two handicaps, 12 with three, and only 1 with four.

Of the 30 children with reactive behavior disorders, 8 had no defects and 14 had damage in only one area. The remaining 8 youngsters with reactive disorders had two or more defects.

Ninety-one children were diagnosed as being retarded, either alone or in combination with another psychiatric disorder. Only 2 of these youngsters had no physical defects. The largest number of retardates, 31, had physical defects in three areas while another 25 had four handicaps. Of the remaining retarded children, 18 had two and 15 had one area of defect. It appears, therefore, that in this sample of children, mental retardation was characteristically associated with multiple physical defects.

These findings, in general, were what one would expect. The high correlation between mental retardation and physical impairment would suggest that retardation occurs when there has been virological invasion of the central nervous system concurrent with virological interference with other developing organs in the fetus.

In considering the data somewhat differently—taking the number of physical defects as primary and the psychiatric diagnoses as associated findings—some other issues are highlighted.

TABLE 14

PSYCHIATRIC DIAGNOSIS AND NUMBER OF PHYSICAL DEFECTS PRESENT

N	Psychiatric Diagnosis	Number of Defect Areas				
		None	One	Two	Three	Four
118	No Psychiatric Disorder	40	41	24	12	1
30	Reactive Behavior Disorder	8	14	4	3	1
2	Cerebral Dysfunction		1	1		
1	Cerebral Dysfunction + Mental Retardation—unspecified				1	
1	Cerebral Dysfunction + Mental Retardation—mild				1	
1	Cerebral Dysfunction + Mental Retardation—severe				1	
1	Mental Retardation—unspecified				1	
7	Mental Retardation—borderline	1	3	2	1	
7	Mental Retardation—mild		1	2	3	1
13	Mental Retardation—moderate		2	3	5	3
26	Mental Retardation—severe		3	6	7	10
11	Mental Retardation—profound			1	4	6
1	Autism				1	
1	Partial Syndrome of Autism		1			
1	Cerebral Dysfunction + Mental Retardation—mild + Reactive Behavior Disorder		1			
1	Cerebral Dysfunction + Mental Retardation—moderate + Reactive Behavior Disorder				1	
2	Reactive Behavior Disorder + Mental Retardation—borderline		1		1	
2	Reactive Behavior Disorder + Mental Retardation—moderate	1				1
1	Reactive Behavior Disorder + Mental Retardation—severe					1
2	Mental Retardation—unspecified + Autism		1		1	
2	Mental Retardation—borderline + Autism				1	1
1	Mental Retardation—moderate + Autism		1			
3	Mental Retardation—severe + Autism			1	1	1
1	Mental Retardation—profound + Autism				1	
3	Mental Retardation—unspecified + Partial Syndrome of Autism		1	1	1	
3	Mental Retardation—moderate + Partial Syndrome of Autism			2		1
1	Cerebral Dysfunction + Mental Retardation—mild + Partial Syndrome of Autism		1			
243	Total	50	72	47	47	27

Fifty youngsters had no apparent physical defects. Of these 40 (80%) were well adapted behaviorally. Eight children had reactive disorders, a proportion that reflects the usual incidence in children this age. Two physically normal children were retarded, and this 4% prevalence is somewhat higher than the usual 2-3% prevalence. Given the small size of this subsample, however, this is not a significant variation.

Of the 72 children with one physical defect, only 41 (57%) showed good behavioral adaptation. Fourteen (19%) had reactive behavior disorders alone. With two exceptions, the remainder of these children with one physical defect (15, or 20%) were mentally retarded, either alone or in combination with symptoms of cerebral dysfunction, reactive behavior disorder, or some degree of autism. One of the exceptions had a single diagnosis of cerebral dysfunction and the other had a partial syndrome of autism.

The prevalence of psychiatric disorders increases still further in the 47 children with two defects. Only half (24) displayed well-adapted age-appropriate behavior. Of the rest, 18 (38%) were mentally retarded, often to a moderate to profound degree, either alone or combined with autism or partial syndrome of autism. Four children (8%) had reactive behavior disorders and one child had cerebral dysfunction.

Another 47 children had defects in three areas. Twelve (24%) were free of psychiatric pathology and 3 (6%) had reactive behavior disorders. The remaining youngsters, with the exception of one autistic child, were retarded, usually to a moderate to profound degree, and several had additional symptoms of cerebral dysfunction or autism.

Of the 27 study children with defects in four areas, only 1 had no psychiatric pathology and 1 had a reactive behavior disorder. All the others were retarded, most commonly to a severe or profound degree. Three of the retardates showed symptoms of autism or partial syndrome of autism.

The correspondence between psychiatric disorder and physical impairment shows up clearly in these children. As the number of physical handicaps increases, a youngster becomes more and more likely to display coexistent behavioral pathology. However, the impressive fact that 37 children who had two or more areas of physical defect were free of psychiatric disorders cautions against assuming a necessary relationship between physical and behavioral sequelae. To emphasize this, it is worthwhile looking at Wanda, a child with four defect areas and good behavioral adaptation.

She was described in the interview reports as a four-year-old, alert, expressive black girl who had two older brothers. The parents were separated, and the mother had custody of the children. The mother had completed three years of college. She was on welfare at the time of the interview. Wanda's mother had had rubella (accompanied by a rash and fever) during her first trimester of pregnancy. The child's clinical manifestations of rubella included severe bilateral deafness, bilateral microphthalmia and myopia, bilateral retinal pigmentation, congenital heart disease (patent ductus arteriosis, status post ligation; pulmonary artery stenosis; sinus rhythm 1A), and bilateral talipes valgus. In addition she was asthmatic, a condition unrelated to rubella. Wanda had worn a hearing aid since she was two years old and glasses since she was 3½.

Although unable to form any words clearly, Wanda did babble and gesture a lot during both the psychological and psychiatric interviews. She seemed very much interested in the people around her and their reactions to what she did. She appeared happy and outgoing, and reacted appropriately in her play performance. She performed on an average level of intelligence, completing successfully the "discrimination of forms" at the four-year level. From material gathered during the parental interview it appeared that Wanda's behavior at home and school was also fully competent within the limitations imposed by her visual and hearing defects and that she had good affective relatedness.

The behavioral data we collected also appeared to indicate a direct correspondence between number of defects and the severity of psychiatric pathology, but this, too, was not a necessary relation. This is illustrated in the case of Ira, a five-year-old boy who was abandoned by his parents at birth and had been living with foster parents since he was three months of age. He saw his natural parents about twice a year when they came to visit him and appeared to have an affectionate relationship with his foster family. His rubella defects included congenital heart disease (status post ligation of patent ductus arteriosis with persistence of a possible pulmonic stenosis or ventricular septal defect), bilateral cataracts (post operative), bilateral microphthalmia and rubella retinopathy, mild hearing loss in the left and profound loss in the right ear, and mild, but true, clubfoot. He wore hearing aids (although his hearing was reported to be the same with or without them) and eyeglasses, which gave him functional vision for large and small objects.

Although Ira was not seen for a psychiatric interview, the data obtained from the behavioral descriptions in the parent interviews and his performance during psychological testing made possible a diagnosis of reactive behavior disorder. He appeared to be a hyperactive boy, somewhat impulsive and undisciplined. His foster parents permitted Ira to run the household and tended to infantilize him. For example, they did not demand that he dress himself, and continued to keep him in a crib and to have him use a toilet-training seat even though he was perfectly capable of servicing himself and sleeping in a full-sized bed. Their lack of structured demands appeared mainly responsible for his difficult behavior. Ira attended a nursery school for normal children and his teachers reported that though he refused to dress himself he was not unmanageable or overly destructive.

He cooperated with the examiner's requests during the psychological testing session, but did not show any interest or curiosity in the test materials or toys in the playroom. He obtained an IQ of 76, which was considered minimal because of his inattention to demands made of him; he probably functioned in the low-average range of intelligence.

COMPARISON OF RUBELLA CHILDREN WITH AND WITHOUT
PHYSICAL DEFECTS

Fifty of the children in the study had, when we saw them, no apparent physical defects as sequelae of congenital rubella. Whether they will continue to be "well babies" or whether some of them will later come to demonstrate the consequences of congenital rubella cannot be determined at this time. It is only since the children of the 1964 epidemic have come under study that the continuing nature of fetal rubella infection was ascertained. The repercussions cannot be definitively categorized without long-term follow-up of these youngsters. It should be recalled that after the World War I epidemic of encephalitis lethargica it was often ten or more years before young adults, infected in childhood, developed delayed sequelae such as oculogyric crises and Parkinsonism.

Isolating our nonhandicapped group and pooling all the children with one or more defects allowed us to emphasize the correlation between physical and behavioral disorders. Table 15 compares the psychiatric diagnoses in the two groups.

While 80% of the physically intact youngsters were judged free of behavioral pathology, only 40% of the physically damaged youngsters were classified as having no psychiatric disorder. Two intact children were retarded (4%) while the prevalence of intellectual deficits was 46% in those who had physical defects.

It is interesting that the incidence of reactive behavior disorders is higher in the non-damaged children (18%) than in the handicapped youngsters (14.5%). Possibly, the behavioral deviations that in these preschool children appeared reactive to stress may later turn out to be early signs of cerebral dysfunction when cognitive and adaptive demands become more complicated. As was mentioned in the previous chapter, this has happened in one child seen at the request of the Rubella Birth Defect Evaluation Project three years after his initial evaluation by us.

TABLE 15

PSYCHIATRIC DIAGNOSES OF PHYSICALLY INTACT AND PHYSICALLY
DAMAGED CHILDREN (N = 243)

	No Physical Defects N = 50		With Physical Defects N = 193	
	N	%	N	%
No Psychiatric Disorder	40	80.0	78	40.4
Cerebral Dysfunction	0	0.0	8	4.1
Reactive Behavior Disorder	9	18.0	28	14.5
Autism	0	0.0	10	5.2
Partial Syndrome of Autism	0	0.0	8	4.1
Mental Retardation (unspecified)	0	0.0	7	3.6
Mental Retardation (borderline)	1	2.0	10	5.2
Mental Retardation (mild)	0	0.0	10	5.2
Mental Retardation (moderate)	1	2.0	19	9.9
Mental Retardation (severe)	0	0.0	31	16.0
Mental Retardation (profound)	0	0.0	12	6.2
Total*	51	102.0	221	114.4

* Adds up to more than the number of children and more than 100% as double diagnoses are recorded separately.

Whether this will or will not be true of others in the group remains to be determined by follow-up studies.

In all the other diagnostic categories—cerebral dysfunction, autism, partial syndrome of autism, mental retardation—children who had sustained physical damage after fetal infection were the sole representatives, except for one borderline and one moderate retardate from the well group.

When we looked at the individual diagnoses of children with and without physical defects, the basic pattern described above still pertained (see Table 16). It thus appears that significant distortions of thought processes, delays in cognitive advances, and inability to relate meaningfully to the environment in an age-appropriate manner have occurred, for the most part, in children who have physical signs of virological invasion of various body systems. This close association lends weight to the possibility, raised independently by those investigating visual and auditory

TABLE 16

PSYCHIATRIC DIAGNOSES (ALL COMBINATIONS)   N = 243

	No Physical Defect N = 50		With Physical Defect N = 193	
	N	%	N	%
No Psychiatric Disorder	40	80.0	78	40.4
Cerebral Dysfunction	0	0.0	2	1.0
Cerebral Dysfunction + Mental Retardation	0	0.0	3	1.6
Reactive Behavior Disorder	8	16.0	22	11.4
Autism	0	0.0	1	0.5
Partial Syndrome of Autism	0	0.0	1	0.5
Mental Retardation—unspecified	0	0.0	1	0.5
Mental Retardation—borderline	1	2.0	6	3.1
Mental Retardation—mild	0	0.0	7	3.6
Mental Retardation—moderate	0	0.0	13	6.7
Mental Retardation—severe	0	0.0	26	13.5
Mental Retardation—profound	0	0.0	11	5.7
Reactive Behavior Disorder + Cerebral Dysfunction + Mental Retardation	0	0.0	2	1.0
Reactive Behavior Disorder + Mental Retardation—borderline	0	0.0	2	1.0
Reactive Behavior Disorder + Mental Retardation—moderate	1	2.0	1	0.5
Reactive Behavior Disorder + Mental Retardation—severe	0	0.0	1	0.5
Mental Retardation—unspecified + Autism	0	0.0	2	1.0
Mental Retardation—borderline + Autism	0	0.0	2	1.0
Mental Retardation—moderate + Autism	0	0.0	1	0.5
Mental Retardation—severe + Autism	0	0.0	3	1.6
Mental Retardation—profound + Autism	0	0.0	1	0.5
Mental Retardation—unspecified + Partial Syndrome of Autism	0	0.0	3	1.6
Mental Retardation—moderate + Partial Syndrome of Autism	0	0.0	3	1.6
Cerebral Dysfunction + Mental Retardation + Partial Syndrome of Autism	0	0.0	1	0.5

defects, that in some cases there may be central damage leading to the end-organ defect.

RELATION OF KIND AND NUMBER OF PHYSICAL DEFECT TO PSYCHIATRIC DIAGNOSIS

Hearing Defects Alone

Hearing loss was the unique defect in 65 children. Most of them (47) had a severe loss of hearing while 14 had a moderate loss. The four youngsters considered to have an "unspecified" loss represented those children whose responses on repeated audiological examinations were so uncertain and/or contradictory as to make their degree of impairment moot.

Half of the children with moderate hearing losses were without psychiatric disorders. Similarly, approximately two-thirds of the youngsters with severe hearing losses (31 of 47) also were adaptively intact. In both cases, the largest groups of children with behavioral deviations had reactive behavior disorders, with the remainder spread among the various subcategories of mental retardation with and without other psychiatric findings. One child had a partial syndrome of autism without retardation. These findings are tabulated in Table 17.

Visual Defects Alone

In most cases, visual defects did not occur in isolation—there were only 4 youngsters in this category, two with severe, and two with moderate impairment. However, the psychiatric casualty rate in this group was high. Two were severely retarded, one had a reactive behavior disorder, and only one was free of behavioral pathology.

Single Cardiac or Neurological Defects

The one study child whose only defect was neurological was mildly retarded. Of the two youngsters whose only defect was cardiological, one had no psychiatric disorder and one had a reactive behavior disorder.

TABLE 17

PSYCHIATRIC DIAGNOSIS IN CHILDREN WITH HEARING DEFECTS

Psychiatric Diagnosis	Unspecified Hearing Loss (N = 4)	Moderate Hearing Loss (N = 14)	Severe Hearing Loss (N = 47)
No Psychiatric Disorder	1	7	31
Reactive Behavior Disorder	2	3	7
Cerebral Dysfunction			1
Autism			
Partial Syndrome of Autism			1
Mental Retardation—borderline			3
Mental Retardation—moderate			2
Mental Retardation—severe		1	
Cerebral Dysfunction + Mental Retardation + Partial Syndrome of Autism	1		
Cerebral Dysfunction + Mental Retardation + Reactive Behavior Disorder		1	
Reactive Behavior Disorder + Mental Retardation—borderline		1	
Mental Retardation—unspecified + Partial Syndrome of Autism		1	
Mental Retardation—unspecified + Autism			1
Mental Retardation—moderate + Autism			1

DOUBLE DEFECTS

There were 47 children in the study with defects in two areas. They were classified in 17 subgroups, 8 of which contained only one child. The details of the psychiatric findings in these groups are given in Appendix A. Here we have considered only pooled data, considering the kinds of defects but not their severity.

Hearing and Visual Impairment

Fourteen youngsters had combined hearing and visual losses of varying severity. Six of these children had no psychiatric disorder, six were retarded, and two combined with retardation a partial syndrome of autism.

Hearing and Neurological Impairment

Eighteen youngsters with impaired hearing also had neurological findings. Of these, eight had no psychiatric disorder, two had reactive behavior disorders, and one had cerebral dysfunction. The remaining 7 were mentally retarded, and one of this group also had a partial syndrome of autism.

Hearing and Cardiac Impairment

There were ten children who had cardiac defects plus hearing losses. Eight of them had no psychiatric disorder, making this the most benign combination of handicaps in terms of presence of behavioral disturbance. One youngster had a reactive behavior disorder and one child was diagnosed as severely retarded and autistic.

Other Double Defects

Only one child had visual and neurological defects and two others had visual and cardiac defects. Two youngsters had neurological and cardiac defects. This small representation permitted us to make no generalizations about their varying psychiatric diagnoses.

TRIPLE DEFECTS

Hearing and Visual and Neurological

Eleven children had a combination of hearing, visual, and neurological defects. Only two of these youngsters had no behavioral pathology. The rest were all retarded, and two of this group had additional symptoms of cerebral dysfunction and one also had a partial syndrome of autism.

Hearing and Visual and Cardiac

Of the seventeen children with these three defects, two had no psychiatric disorders. Three youngsters had only reactive behavior disorders. There was one autistic child of normal intelligence. The remaining 11 children were retarded, and two of them were also autistic.

Hearing and Neurological and Cardiac

This particular defect combination was found in 15 children of whom eight were behaviorally normal. All the rest had some degree of intellectual deficit; in two cases this was associated with additional symptoms of cerebral dysfunction and in one case with autism.

Visual and Neurological and Cardiac

Only four children had this particular combination of defects and all of them were retarded.

Quadruple Defects: Hearing and Visual and Neurological and Cardiac

As we have described earlier, only one of the 27 youngsters with defects in four areas was well-adjusted behaviorally and another one had only a reactive behavior disorder. All of the rest were mentally retarded, frequently to a severe or profound degree. Two of the retarded children were also autistic, and one also had a partial syndrome of autism.

CHILDREN MOST AT RISK

It is clear that as the number of areas of defect increases so does the risk for psychiatric disorder. However, this risk is also related to the *kind* of handicap the child has. Although hearing defects were most common in this group of youngsters, only 41.7% of those with hearing loss alone or in combination with either or both cardiac and neurological defects had psychiatric disorders. In contrast, although these handicaps were much less frequently found, 81.8% of those with visual loss alone or combined with either or both cardiac and neurological defects had behavioral pathology. And, if we isolate children with both hearing and visual defects, either as their only handicap or combined with one other physical symptom, 76.2% had psychiatric disorders.

It thus appears that the risk for psychiatric disorder is particularly prominent in children with visual loss or a combination of visual and hearing losses, irrespective of their other physical handicaps. This vulnerability of the "deaf-blind" rubella child is further discussed in Chapter 6.

5

Areas of Behavioral Disturbance

CATEGORIZING THE BEHAVIORAL DISORDERS found in the rubella children gave us a broad picture of how they were functioning. We also wanted to know if there was such a thing as a "behavioral" rubella syndrome.

When pediatricians speak of the "expanded rubella syndrome" they are referring to a wide range of physical characteristics and disabilities observed in children who were fetally infected. As knowledge of the physical sequelae of congenital rubella has increased, it has become obvious that simply calling a youngster a "rubella child" does not tell us what he is like. This term opens for consideration a large number of possible consequences, but it cannot be assumed that the child will necessarily display any or all of them. The diversity of sequelae is all that one can be sure of.

We believed that the same thing would be true of the behaviors shown by the rubella children—that is, there would be a wide variety of patterns, so that the knowledge that a youngster had rubella would not definitively describe his behavioral pattern. Nevertheless, it would still be important to take note of behaviors that deviated from the norm since, as with physical deviances, these would be critically implicated in methods of parental handling.

In order to examine the areas in which rubella children showed behavioral disturbances, we pooled the descriptions of each child in the study, regardless of his diagnosis. The deviant behaviors discussed were not limited to children with psychiatric disorders. They also occurred in children whose overall adaptation was not considered deviant. The finding of a disturbance in a specific area of behavior did not necessarily signify general pathology, either because there were only isolated examples of such deviations or, if multiple, they were present only to a mild degree. Thus, while they represented inconveniences to the parents or reflected a need for special planning or handling, such special arrangements were not extensive and the youngster's behavior as a whole was basically normal.

Furthermore, since the diagnosis of a behavior disorder is always a statement about a child's functioning within a specific environment, differences in parent handling also played a role in differentiating between behavioral deviations and psychiatric disorders. Well-organized and understanding parents might manage most of their child's deviant, "nuisance" behavior so it was kept in the background and did not become a full-blown behavior problem. With other parents, whose handling was inconsistent or antagonistic, the same nuisance behaviors might become so prominent and disrupting that the child was given a psychiatric diagnosis.

For these reasons, the presence or absence of psychiatric pathology was not taken into account in considering areas of behavioral disturbance. Rather, the focus was on specific deviations beyond the range of normalcy. Neither the highly active child nor the motorically quiet child was tallied if this activity was within the boundaries of normal variance. Similarly, variations in attention span, distractibility, ease of adaptability, and other qualities of the individual at either end of the normal spectrum were not considered deviations.

The description of behavioral patterns was obtained from written observations of the rubella children's home activities and of their functioning during scheduled examinations as well as from parent interview reports. The home interviewer, social worker, psychologist, and psychiatrist recorded their individual descriptions of the child's observed activity, and each of them requested parents to illustrate general statements with specific examples of the child's activity.

The behaviors thus recorded were divided into the categories that were used in the New York Longitudinal Study (Thomas, et al., 1968). In the present study, we added another category, dressing, which was of major concern to the parents of our rubella children. Thus, the classification of reported behavioral difficulties embraces 12 specific areas: sleep, feeding and eating, dressing, elimination, mood, discipline, motor activity, habits and rituals, somatic, speech, social relationships, and learning. To these categories we have appended "other behavioral deviations," which for the most part reflect the children's immaturity and fears.

Some behaviors were clearly referable to only one category. In other instances, where criteria were debatable, the definitions used were those of the New York Longitudinal Study and associated clinical research in order to maintain comparability. Illustrations for each category are given in Appendix B.

In the records of 234 children (all but the nine who were institutionalized) there were sufficient descriptive data from which to isolate behavioral deviations. We made a separate record of observed and reported information, since some behaviors, such as eating or elimination problems, would not be observed during

TABLE 18

AREAS OF BEHAVIORAL DISTURBANCE
(N = 234)

	Observed No.	Observed %	Reported No.	Reported %	Total (Duplications Eliminated)* No.	%
Sleep	0	0.0	108	46.2	108	46.2
Feeding	1	0.4	125	53.4	125	53.4
Dressing	1	0.4	61	26.1	62	26.4
Elimination	4	1.7	83	35.5	86	36.8
Mood	69	29.4	153	65.4	168	71.8
Discipline	69	29.4	134	57.2	149	63.7
Motor Activity	98	41.9	90	38.5	128	54.7
Habits & Rituals	63	26.9	142	60.7	155	66.2
Somatic	17	7.3	9	3.8	20	8.5
Speech	172	73.5	142	60.7	195	83.3
Social Relationships	65	27.7	111	47.4	132	56.4
Learning	4	1.7	7	3.0	11	4.7
Other Behavioral Deviations	82	35.0	160	68.3	180	76.9

* If the same behavioral disturbance was both reported and observed, it is listed only once in the total.

an office visit. Where behavior deviations were both observed and reported, they were recorded in both places, but only counted once in the total summary (see Table 18).

It should be noted that our discussion of the behavioral deviations found in the rubella children is basically qualitative, even though we have tabulated the incidence of problems. This is because we have little quantitative information on the specific behaviors of nonhandicapped youngsters in our other studies. The need for complete behavioral descriptions of children with normal sensorial capacity has not arisen unless they have developed psychiatric disorders. Thus, only the clinical cases in the New York Longitudinal Study were tabulated according to the detailed behavioral inventory. As a result, we can use only those data plus our general clinical experience as reference points for the discussion of the rubella children which follows.

AREAS OF SPECIFIC BEHAVIORAL DEVIATIONS

Sleep—Forty-six per cent of the rubella children had sleep problems, an unusually high frequency of this kind of disorder, even for preschool youngsters. The specific problems mentioned by the parents were often related to unusual sleep patterns. Many children went to bed very late, woke up during the night, walked around the house at night after being put to bed, or went into their parents' bed.

It was interesting that nightmares, usually a prominent and common sleep problem in children this age, were rarely reported by the parents of the rubella children. This underrepresentation could be due to the fact that so many of the children could not speak about a disturbing dream because they were deaf. However, the mothers rarely remarked that their children woke up screaming and crying during the night, a nightmare sign within the capacity of deaf youngsters.

Feeding and Eating—Fifty-three per cent of the rubella children had difficulties in the area of eating. By contrast, in physically normal youngsters, eating problems are found infrequently. The parents of the rubella children complained that their offspring were unable to progress from drinking fluids to chewing solids and that they often refused to learn to eat. These problems were found in all the social classes represented in our sample.

There may have been a physical basis for these difficulties in some of the youngsters. Among the neurological signs found in the group as a whole, swallowing difficulties were not uncommon. Other centers studying children born after the 1964 epidemic have reported similar difficulties.

Dressing—More than one-fourth of the children displayed deviances in one or another aspect of dressing. As in eating, some of the difficulties reflected lack of self-care ability due to retardation or motor incoordination. Other problems arose when the youngsters insisted that parental servicing be perpetuated. Some children had phobic reactions to clothing or showed easy irritability to being dressed, particularly when they had to have tight garments pulled over their heads or had to hold their feet still while shoes were being put on and tied. We have speculated on a number of possible reasons for such difficulties. In some instances, the child's activity level may have played a part—a youngster with a high activity level may have found it extremely disagreeable to hold still for dressing. Some children with sensory damage may have developed a very low threshold to tactile sensation to compensate for visual and hearing deficits. In other children, such hyperreactivity may be the first manifestation of cerebral dysfunction.

Elimination—As in the three prior categories, difficulties in this area were made known through parental reports; there was little opportunity to observe these problems directly either on home visits or during office examinations. Here, too, the large number of children with deviations (37% of the sample) was noteworthy.

With all children, including those without sensory defect, toilet-training is considered an important developmental milestone. It represents a major occupation of the parents during a youngster's second year of life. Innumerable advice-giving articles are written on the subject, and there is extensive theorizing about the psychological effects of parent-child interactions during toilet-training.

Parents of the rubella children wished to complete this phase of training as smoothly as possible, but they often had to face special problems resulting from the child's specific defects. If the child was retarded, toilet-training would be delayed. Irregularity in biological functioning further added to the difficulty of teaching some youngsters to signal their impending needs. Problems in oral communication due to hearing defects would certainly help account for the high proportion of children with reported elimination difficulties. This is clearly one of the areas in which parents of rubella children need special assistance.

The incidence of such problems, while understandable in terms of the physical and intellectual capacities of the children, also had to be evaluated in terms of its meaning to the parents. In general, the parents were sensitive to any sign which would alert a bystander that theirs was a deviant child. Items associated with lack of toilet-training were high on this list. Frequently, too, these factors influenced the parents' plans, so that they did not take the child on outings because they felt unable to cope with the stares of strangers.

Mood—Mood difficulties were found in almost three-fourths (72%) of the children. The psychiatric and psychological evaluations enabled us to observe some of these social deviations. Separation anxiety and clinging or withdrawn behavior were especially prominent. Mothers reported temper tantrums, screaming without provocation, and affective deviances as mood disturbances at home.

Some of these behaviors may represent early symptoms of cerebral dysfunction. Even though temper tantrums are not uncommon in normal preschool children, one cannot be sure that they are not the first sign of an impulse disorder in these vulnerable youngsters. The validity of this supposition can be confirmed only when follow-up studies are done.

In other instances, these mood deviations may reflect the high degree of frustration felt by children with hearing deficits who cannot express their needs and desires in speech. Furthermore, these youngsters may be receiving only incomplete signals from their parents, due to losses or fluctuations in their hearing ability, and they may therefore have found it difficult to learn an appropriate repertoire of adaptive behaviors. Because their understanding of parental demands is only partial, they could make no clear distinction between behavior that will be rewarded and that which will be reprimanded. To the parents, this then showed up as "peculiar" moods or deviant affect.

Discipline—This was one of the greatest problem areas, as indicated by the fact that 64 per cent (almost two-thirds) of the children were considered to be deviant in this area. The whole question of disciplining the rubella children presented the parents with many dilemmas. Sometimes they were not sure if the child could either hear or understand what they told him to do and they hesitated to punish him for infractions of rules of which he might not even be aware. In situations where they knew the child could comprehend their requests, parents were also reluctant to impose disciplinary measures. They often said, "Is it right to punish a child who is handicapped and already punished enough?" even though they knew his incorporation into the larger society around him depended on his ability to take directions.

The behaviors that evoked parental concern about discipline were largely the children's destructive and disruptive activities. Frequently, the consequences of the youngster's behaviors were more worrisome than the degree to which they were undisciplined. For example, impulsive behavior that did not endanger the child's personal safety or result in the destruction of his sister's homework or a neighbor's antique vase could be overlooked or ignored. However, if the child could not be trained to keep from darting into the street or from leaning out of windows, parental vigilance and control were mandatory. This was not "overprotection," but realism; severe motor restrictions on the child might be an appropriate disciplinary measure that would keep him from getting hurt. Yet, as a result, the child often came to experience life as filled with external prohibitions and he might build up a number of defensive behaviors such as negativeness, fearfulness, or a sense that his parents will always take charge and interpret the world to him at every step.

There were no easy answers to questions about how to handle

the child. Both discipline and the lack of discipline could cause further difficulties, and the parents' dilemma was a real one.

Motor Activity—More than half of the children (55%) displayed deviant motor activity, and these behaviors were slightly more often observed than reported. Parental complaints about the youngster's motoric behavior usually centered on examples of hyperactivity, probably because it led to management problems. In this way, this particular motor deviance came to be given undue prominence: because of its intrusive nature, it was always reported. By contrast, reports of hypoactivity only came out under close questioning. To the parents, the hypoactive youngster was the "good" child, who sat for hours playing quietly and not bothering anyone. Their descriptions led to probing about the quality of this "goodness," but the parents did not see it spontaneously as a sign of unusually little activity.

Members of the study team observed peculiarities of gait, motoric incompetence, drooling, and tremors that were not always identified by the parents. There were a number of possible explanations for this discrepancy. In the course of daily living, the parents may have become accustomed to these aspects of a child's functioning. Or, since so many youngsters had several gross handicaps, such peculiarities may have been seen as not warranting primary attention. Then, too, the parents' recognition of the child's limitations in motor competence may have lowered their expectations, so that specific defects were no longer recorded in their minds.

Habits and Rituals—Habits and rituals were reported for two-thirds of the children. This may be related both to the high incidence of children with sensory defects and the high proportion of mentally retarded children in this study. Many authors have reported that children with visual losses often display "blindisms," various forms of self-stimulation whose cause is unknown. Among the blindisms shown by the rubella youngsters were poking the eyes, waving fingers before the eyes, rocking the head sideways, and staring at lights.

Other rituals in the rubella children resembled those found in mentally retarded youngsters (Chess and Hassibi, 1970) whose overall adaptation was, in general, adequate. Among these behaviors were flapping of the arms, rocking, and other repetitive, aimless motor activities.

Another habit frequently mentioned by the parents was the rubella children's tendency to smell all objects. While it was acceptable to smell food before eating it, as many children do, these youngsters also had to smell toys, the pages of a book, people's feet, and almost everything else—behavior that the parents felt was unacceptable.

The parents found these habits and rituals both difficult to understand and a source of embarrassment. The activities were very visible, and they quickly identified a child as deviant and could make him the object of teasing. As a result, parents put much effort into trying to eliminate these habits, usually to no avail.

Somatic—Somatic reactions were relatively few. They consisted mainly of gastrointestinal reactions, such as gagging and vomiting in response to unpleasant odors. Although a hyperreactivity to smell is found occasionally in children with intact sensory capacities, in these rubella children it may reflect a compensatory sensation. The sense of smell may be more highly developed in children whose hearing and vision is faulty, and this, in turn, would cause them to gag more frequently in response to unpleasant odors.

Speech—Eighty-three per cent of the rubella children had speech difficulties. The relation between hearing loss and speech disturbances is logical, and many of the deaf children were in this category. It is noteworthy that several of the well babies without defined hearing deficits also had speech defects. These deviations, which were unexplained by physical damage, may be transitory maturational lags or they may be the first indications of cerebral dysfunction. Many of the parents of the non-deaf children (and some of the deaf, too) explained their offspring's speech deviations in terms of a familial developmental pattern. While this may prove to be correct in some cases, the group of children with these defects was too large for this explanation to hold good for all. For some youngsters these speech problems may be a prognostic sign of cerebral dysfunction that will become obvious at a later age when they face more complex demands.

Social Relations—More than 50 per cent of the children showed some difficulty in social relationships. The problems included aggressive acts, such as hitting, kicking, biting, and withdrawal from other children. Many of these "acting-out" behaviors were explainable by the fact of mental retardation, but this did not make them any more acceptable. The parents could be objective about some aspects of their retarded child's functioning, and knew not to expect him to dress or feed himself since youngsters of his developmental age did not have these self-care abilities. But, they were reasonably concerned about the child's interpersonal behavior. Although a normal child of the same developmental age could fight with a peer, since they were matched in size, aggression in the retardate had to be controlled. Even though his actions were appropriate to his developmental age, his size and strength made him dangerous to the younger children with whom he played.

Withdrawal from others, also reported by the parents, was equally deviant behavior, but it caused less parental concern, since it did not have to be dealt with in these preschoolers. If the child chose not to participate in group activities, he could be left alone on the sidelines at this stage without much ado.

Learning—This category deals primarily with problems in formal or academic learning situations. One would not expect to find many learning deviations in this group of preschool youngsters.

The parents generally made few formal learning demands because of the children's handicaps, and the youngsters had not quite reached the chronological age at which academic demands would usually be made. It is interesting to note, however, that the Rubella Birth Defect Evaluation Project, in their follow-ups of the children, have found that learning problems are showing up in a number of them as they grow older.

Other Behavioral Deviations—This category included behaviors reflecting immaturity, fears, and other isolated symptoms. In the subgroup of immature behaviors, more deviances were observed by study personnel than were reported by parents, thus reaffirming the likelihood that parents have so readjusted their expectations to a lower level that they are no longer able to judge age-appropriateness and do not identify some of the children's behaviors as immature.

Almost half of the parents reported that their offspring had specific fears, such as of water, thunder, cars, masks. These were not in themselves unusual, but their high incidence and the intensity with which they were expressed were notable.

At the same time, however, parents reported their concern that the child who had specific fears frequently lacked an ordinary sense of caution and hence did not exercise proper fearfulness in regard to experiences that had already proved harmful. Thus, one youngster repeatedly jumped from the top of a flight of stairs, expecting his parents to catch him each time. These parents and others expressed the wish that the youngsters would have "proper" or "normal" fears.

BEHAVIORAL DEVIATIONS AND THE PRESENCE OR ABSENCE OF PSYCHIATRIC DISORDERS

As we have said, the presence of a behavioral deviation did not necessarily indicate the presence of a psychiatric disorder unless the number and/or severity of deviances added up to a

TABLE 19

AREAS OF BEHAVIORAL DISTURBANCE
(Comparison of Children with No Psychiatric Disorder and
Those with Psychiatric Disorder)

	All Children (N = 234)		Children with No Psychiatric Disorder (N = 118)		Children with Psychiatric Disorder (N = 116)	
	N	%	N	%	N	%
Sleep	108	46.2	44	37.3	64	55.1
Feeding	125	53.4	49	41.5	76	65.5
Dressing	62	26.4	12	10.2	50	43.1
Elimination	86	36.8	15	12.7	71	61.2
Mood	168	71.8	63	53.4	105	90.5
Discipline	149	63.7	54	45.8	95	81.9
Motor Activity	128	54.7	34	28.8	94	81.0
Habits & Rituals	155	66.2	56	47.5	99	85.3
Somatic	20	8.5	5	4.2	15	12.9
Speech	195	83.3	87	73.7	108	93.1
Social Relationships	132	56.4	48	40.7	84	72.4
Learning	11	4.7	3	2.5	8	6.9
Other	180	76.9	74	62.7	106	91.4

total adaptational problem. Nevertheless, the child with deviant behavior in some area did present difficulties in management. To highlight what these were, we tabulated these behavioral problems in terms of the presence or absence of a diagnosis. Table 19 gives an overall picture of behavioral deviations with which parents of children with congenital rubella, even when the youngster is psychiatrically normal.

More than half the children with psychiatric disorders were represented in every area of deviation except dressing, somatic, and learning. Over 90% of them had mood and speech problems.

Of the children with no psychiatric disorder, the largest percentage had mood (53.4%) and speech (73.7%) deviances. Other problem areas which involved 25% or more of the non-psychiatric group were, in descending order, habits and rituals (47.5%), discipline (45.8%), feeding (41.5%), social relationships (40.7%), sleep (37.3%) and motor activity (28.8%). In addition, 62.7%

TABLE 20

Behavioral Disturbances and Physical Status

	No Physical Defect N = 50		With Physical Defects N = 184	
	N	%	N	%
Sleep	16	32.0	92	50.0
Feeding	16	32.0	109	59.2
Dressing	8	16.0	54	29.3
Elimination	5	10.0	81	44.0
Mood	25	50.0	143	77.7
Discipline	26	52.0	123	66.8
Motor Activity	12	24.0	116	63.0
Habits & Rituals	21	42.0	134	72.8
Somatic	1	2.0	19	10.3
Speech	18	36.0	177	96.2
Social Relationships	24	48.0	108	58.7
Learning	0	0.0	11	6.0
Other	37	74.0	146	79.3
Average Number Complaints per case	4.2	....	7.2	....

of these psychiatrically normal youngsters showed immaturity or fears.

It is clear from these data that daily management of even the relatively well adapted rubella child requires considerable planning and special awareness from parents. Even such a child is not necessarily free of problems.

Many of the deviations found in these children may not yet be indicative of psychiatric disorder because of their stage of development and socialization. It is possible that at a later age, when environmental demands become more complicated, some of these children will exhibit full psychiatric disorders. How much of their symptomatology now is predictive of future disorder can only be determined with follow-up studies.

BEHAVIORAL DEVIATIONS AND PHYSICAL STATUS

It was also of interest to compare the incidence of behavioral deviations in children with and without physical defects (see

Table 20). Children with defects were found to have behavioral disturbances in every category much more frequently than the non-damaged youngsters. This finding further emphasizes the accumulated stresses on the families of these rubella children and it highlights the fact that the physical sequelae are only one of the many problems they must face in daily interaction with the damaged child.

6

Assessing Intellectual Development

THE CONCEPT OF DEVELOPMENT refers to "those changes in behavior that normally occur with an increase in the chronological age of the child" (Spiker, 1966). This operational definition implies that there is a sequence of steps through which each child passes as part of his growth process. However, the age at which these steps are taken differs considerably from one youngster to the next. And the rate at which the changes occur may vary widely not only from child to child, but also in the same child at various stages. For long periods a child may not appear to be learning any new skills or moving toward the next stage, but at other times he seems to leap from one accomplishment to the next. A child who sits at six months (the average age for this milestone) may not be able to walk unassisted until he is 18 months. Such a deviation from the normal scales is often called a "maturational lag," but this term is only a description used to cover our ignorance and does not explain what is really happening.

The concept of development, as it pertains specifically to this discussion, must be considered together with the concept of intelligence. Defining intelligence is a most difficult task. Some authors hold that intelligence implies ability, what the person can do. Others refer to the child's inborn potentiality, implying that all intelligence is genetically determined. Still others define intelligence as that which an intelligence test measures, i.e. on the Binet Scale, "judgment, common sense, initiative and the ability to adapt oneself . . . to judge well, understand well, reason well" (Terman, 1916).

Because the main defect in the rubella children is sensory loss, we thought that Piaget's conception of intelligence—which follows the child's intellectual growth from infancy onward, starting with the sensorimotor stage—would be a useful approach. Piaget defines intelligence as an on-going process of organization and adaptation. It is an activity that allows the individual to develop a fixed sequence of "schemata," or behavior patterns, through interaction with the environment. The environment provides stimuli which the child must actively assimilate or incorporate in order for his intelligence to develop. This interaction between child and environment is the crucial element in the development of intelligence. To review briefly Piaget's thesis, we must start with the neonate.

At birth, the child already has the sensorimotor capacity for grasping the world around him. He is looking, listening, actively taking in the sights, sounds, and other information available in his immediate environment. From this initial period when he is merely sensing these stimuli, he progresses to a period, at about five months of age, when he shows recognition of familiar objects. Towards the end of his first year, the child begins to display what is commonly called "intelligent behavior," that is, he coordinates his movements in order to achieve a certain goal. The classic example is the baby's searching for an object that has just been shown to him and is then hidden.

During the second year of life, while the child is still in the sensorimotor stage, he develops to the point where he explores the novelty of new situations for their own sake, that is, "he will not only submit to but even provide new results instead of being satisfied merely to reproduce them once they have been revealed fortuitously" (Piaget, 1952). The child "invents" new ways of achieving. By age two, he can accept or dismiss ways of dealing with the world around him without first motorically acting to see what will happen. This ability to represent in his own mind the consequences of an act is possible only if he has had the experiences of using his sensorimotor capacities while he was assimilating environmental stimuli during his first two years of life.

The crucial role of external stimuli in the sensorimotor stage should be underlined here. "The more new things an infant has seen and the more new things he has heard, the more new things he is interested in seeing and hearing; and the more variation in reality he has coped with, the greater is his capacity for coping. Such relationships derive from the concept that change in circumstances is required during the early sensorimotor stage to force the accommodative modifications in schemata and the assimilations that, in combination, constitute development" (Hunt, 1961).

At about age two, "there exists an essential moment in the development of intelligence: the moment when the awareness of relationships is sufficiently advanced to permit a reasoned prevision, that is to say, an invention operated by simple mental combination" (Piaget, 1952). Although this represents a tremendous leap forward for the child, it is simply the next stage in the continuum of developing intelligence. In other words, Piaget believes that the ability to symbolize follows logically from the relationships motorically established in earlier stages. Without this underpinning, further development will be hindered.

These relationships which the young child normally establishes during the sensorimotor stage are highly dependent on seeing and hearing. These senses are the most highly developed and discriminatory in man, and they are the ones that mediate most often between the child and his surrounding environment. Through hearing and seeing, the child locates himself in the world and defines his relationship to the objects and people around him. Although the sense of touch does permit one to explore the environment, it offers only a fragmentary and limited perception, whereas vision allows a direct, complete, and immediate sensation. Furthermore, since humans depend on language for communication, the ability to hear permits the all-essential dialogue no other sense can provide.

Children, from birth, produce sounds. In the normal infant, these vocalizations proceed from crying, gurgling, and cooing to babbling, imitative sounds, and his first words. The child who is born deaf also cries and babbles at first. However, without sounds for him to hear and imitate, he will stop vocalizing. As Lewis (1957) has noted, imitation is essential to speech and language development, and the deaf child "will remain mute unless a substitute is found for his absent power of imitating heard speech."

In the world in which we live, language (the ability to speak) is a basic need. It is the means not only for communicating but also for knowing, learning, and perhaps even thinking. As Bertrand Russell put it, "almost all higher intellectual activity is a matter of words, to the nearly total exclusion of everything else" (Russell, 1921). What happens, then, to a child who cannot use or hear words and lives in a world of soundless activity which is inexplicable to him?

Many investigators believe that words are mediators of thinking—that one cannot think without words. They suggest that grasping the logical relationship involved in a situation is much more difficult than understanding the specific content of the situation. They therefore emphasize the necessity for explaining the general principle of the situation to the child. Once the child has had the explanation, he can then apply it to other similar situations and arrive at his own solutions according to the principle. The dependency on using words to give this explanation hardly needs emphasis.

The many studies of the cognitive functioning of deaf children have led to very contradictory conclusions. Some investigators report that deaf children can perform as well as control groups with normal hearing on various tests of intelligence. Other investigators say that the deaf children they studied are so hindered that their fundamental capacity to think and reason is defective. It is possible that some of this confusion has arisen because the extremely heterogeneous nature of the deaf population studied has not been sufficiently differentiated. It is not enough to say that a child is moderately or severely deaf and therefore can be compared to other deaf children in the same general category. Rather, one must carefully consider the etiology, insofar as it distinguishes those who are peripherally deaf from those who have central nervous system damage causing deafness.

If the deafness is due to a lesion in the central nervous system, this basic injury will have multiple ramifications that will not all become manifest at the same time. Though the child appears to be "just" deaf as an infant, other problems may later assert themselves. Specific learning disabilities may become apparent only when the centrally damaged child begins to be confronted with demands for learning. At still a later age, difficulty in abstract thinking may come to play a larger role as the child is expected to be able to generalize and reason. Since these problems appear new when they develop, they are often described as discrete symptoms of maldevelopment at each stage. Actually, they are manifestations of the same central defect. The child's failures, as he grows older, reflect the changes in demands made of him and not basic alterations in his capacities.

We approached the assessment of intellectual development in our sample of deaf children without bias as to whether or not their cognitive functioning would be equivalent to hearing children of the same age. Nevertheless, since it was known that their hearing defects were due to rubella, and that this virus has been found to cause brain damage, we were attentive to specific signs of cognitive difficulties.

In order to find out in broad terms how these children had developed intellectually, psychological testing was necessary. Through the administration of specific tests we could determine both how each individual child was able to perform and how the performance of the group as a whole compared with that of youngsters who had not had rubella.

The selection of an intelligence test involved two major considerations. First, the diversity of physical conditions in our children, ranging from intact youngsters to those with four overwhelming handicaps, meant that the special tests designed for handicapped children were not applicable to all in this group. Moreover, since so many of the children had unique combinations of defects, in terms of both kind and severity, it was practically impossible to select one test that would be exactly suitable for all of them. The use of special tests might have permitted us to tap the potential of each individual child more fully, but it would have prevented us from making relevant comparisons between the children.

Secondly, we felt that since these children, despite their handicaps, would have to live in a world of normal individuals, it was important to assess their functioning against that of nondamaged children, that is, by using scales for normal youngsters. In this way we could get a realistic picture of a youngster's performance in facing the demands of the normal outside world.

Intellectual assessments usually translate a child's functioning into a specific number; this is not a reliable determination for young children, whether normal or handicapped. Assignment of a number is less valuable than a broad determination of the young child's intelligence with relation to the performance of others. "If . . . intelligence is conceived as a *ranking* relative to other children of the same age, then infant tests do seem to be able to predict the children's later standing with respect to his peers" (Elkind, 1967). By defining a child's intelligence in terms of a broad category of functioning rather than a specific number, we are able to get an acceptable picture of his present capacities as well as a more reliable guide to his future intellectual performance.

In planning our study, it soon became apparent that there were few studies of the intellectual development of multihandicapped children. The consensus of reports on children with both auditory and visual defects was that standardized developmental tests should be used, with modifications in their presentation. Weighing all these factors, we decided to use only the Stanford-Binet and Cattell Scales, supplemented by data based on observation of the children and questioning of the mother.

TESTING OF THE CHILDREN

The Stanford-Binet is the most widely used instrument for assessing the intelligence of children. We used Form L-M, Third Revision (Terman and Merrill, 1960). One of the reasons the Binet Scale has been so successful is that it embodies a dynamic approach to intelligence insofar as it looks at total functioning rather than at isolated mental processes. In addition, the Binet provides a situation in which evaluations can be made of motivational and emotional factors that determine the child's use of whatever capacity is being measured.

In trying to keep the standard format of psychological testing, we initially asked the children to go alone into the playroom. In some cases, there were no major difficulties in effecting the separation of the youngsters from their parents, perhaps because the children were used to spending time away from their mothers while attending special classes or clinics. However, some youngsters did not want to enter the playroom or cooperate if they were unaccompanied by a parent. When the mother came with them, they were quite willing to perform.

TABLE 21

EVALUATION OF INTELLIGENCE

Intellectual Level	N	%
Superior	4	2.3
Above Average	17	9.9
Average	53	31.0
Dull normal	23	13.5
Borderline	17	9.9
Mild retardation	6	3.5
Moderate retardation	11	6.4
Severe retardation	15	8.8
Profound retardation	7	4.1
No estimate possible	18	10.5
Total	171	99.9

We therefore decided to see the mother and child together. In addition to providing an atmosphere most conducive to the optimal functioning of the child, this also provided an opportunity to observe the ways the mother and child had found to communicate with each other. Furthermore, it gave us a chance to talk to the mother and to obtain her evaluation of the child's functioning and her estimation of his intelligence.

An attempt was made to obtain an IQ score for each child by administering the Stanford-Binet Intelligence Test (Form L-M) or, in cases of the younger children and those whose intellectual functioning was severely impaired as a result of mental retardation, by administration of the Cattell Infant Scale (Cattell, 1960).

Table 21 shows the distribution of the intelligence levels of the 171 children in the study who were seen for formal psychological testing.

It is generally accepted that in a random population of children from 2% to 3% of the youngsters will be retarded. Here we find that approximately 23% of those tested score in the retarded range. (It should be mentioned that the retarded children analyzed in detail in this chapter are so identified *solely* on

TABLE 22

NUMBER OF DEFECT AREAS AND INTELLECTUAL FUNCTIONING

Number of Defect Areas	Superior & Above Average	Average	Dull Normal	Mental Retardation Borderline & Mild	Mental Retardation Moderate, Severe, Profound
0	12	16	1	1	1
1	5	23	9	8	2
2	4	8	8	6	6
3	0	6	4	4	12
4	0	0	1	4	12
Total*	21	53	23	23	33

* We have tabulated only those children for whom an estimate was possible, 153 of the 171 children tested.

the basis of test scores, whereas the diagnosis of retardation used in the general study was based on test scores, where available, plus a detailed consideration of adaptive behavior. Thus, although the numbers appear discrepant it is only because we are highlighting somewhat different aspects of functioning—actual intelligence test performance as against a range of adaptive behavior observed at home and in other situations.)

The finding of an extraordinarily high percentage of retardation is the most striking aspect of the psychological evaluation. It does not necessarily tell us that this group of children will continue to perform in the retarded range at a later age. However, it does emphasize their tremendous disadvantage in cognitive ability at this time.

Since so many of the youngsters had physical defects, especially in the sensory area, it was important to look at the relationship between the number of defects a child had and his overall area of intellectual functioning (Table 22).

Of the 47 children with physical defects in only one area, 37 (79%) have intellectual levels ranging from dull normal through superior. By contrast, of the 17 children with physical defects in four areas, only 1 child tested in this range whereas the remainder showed some degree of retardation. The data indicate, moreover, that the majority of children with defects in two or fewer areas have at least dull normal intelligence levels while the majority of children with three or four defects function on a retarded level. It is apparent, from Table 22, therefore, that the children's cognitive abilities decrease as the number of physical defects increases.

Nevertheless, it is interesting to note that even among those children with no apparent physical defects there was a higher percentage of retardation than is normally encountered (6% against 3%). One could speculate about the etiology of the higher incidence of retardation in this group. Here again, the possibility of some kind of CNS dysfunction must be considered, although there is no specific finding that proves a link between fetal rubella and brain damage.

Because a child is so dependent on sensory input for his cognitive development it became necessary to note the relationship not only between the number of defects and intellectual functioning but also between the kind of defect and his performance on an intellectual test. Table 23 summarizes our findings.

Hearing defects, by far the most commonly found handicap in this group of rubella children, do not appear to interfere greatly with intellectual performance when they are found in isolation. Of the 42 children with hearing defects alone for whom an estimate could be made, 33 (78.6%) functioned at a dull normal level or above. Similarly, visual defects alone do not hamper intellectual functioning in the two children in our study with this handicap, although the small size of this subsample prevents a full study of this variable. For the same reason, we cannot say anything about those children, only three in number, who have either cardiac or neurological defects alone.

When we examine the intellectual capacities of children with two defects, it becomes apparent that the most severe liability occurs in those with hearing and visual losses. Although the

TABLE 23

KINDS OF DEFECTS AND INTELLECTUAL FUNCTIONING

Intellectual Estimate	Visual Defect Alone	Hearing Defect Alone	Neuro. Alone	Card. Alone	Visual & Hearing	Visual & Neuro. or Card.	Hearing & Neuro or Cardiac	Visual & Hear. w Neuro. or Card.	Neuro. & Card. w Visual or Hear.	Visual, Hearing Neuro., Cardiac
Superior or Above Average	1	3	0	1	1	1	2	0	0	0
Average	1	21	0	1	1	1	6	3	3	0
Dull Normal	0	9	0	0	1	0	6	3	2	1
Mentally Retarded; borderline or mild	0	7	1	0	3	0	2	3	2	4
Mentally Retarded; moderate, severe or profound	0	2	0	0	2	0	5	8	4	11
Total	2	42	1	2	8	2	21	17	11	16

number of youngsters in this subsample is small, almost 63% function at a retarded level, whereas only one-third of those with hearing loss plus either a neurological or cardiac defect score in this range.

Similarly, when we consider the youngsters with three defects, those with a visual and hearing handicap plus one other disability fare less well on intelligence tests than those without this combination of sensory loss. Finally, as we saw earlier, only one child with four handicaps performed on a non-retarded level.

From this table then, it would appear that the deaf-blind rubella child—that is, a child with major difficulties both in visual and hearing areas—no matter what his other physical defects may be, is the one whose cognitive abilities are most limited. This highlights the great disadvantage of the deaf-blind rubella children vis-à-vis even the rubella child with other defects, and calls attention to the need for specific training procedures and remedial techniques that will enhance the use of their residual sensory capacities.

Speech and Hearing

The most important consequence of rubella is deafness. In our sample of 243 children, 65 (26.7%) had hearing defects alone and a further 112 youngsters had hearing loss in combination with other defects. Thus, almost three-fourths of the children presented deafness as a major disability.

Because we are interested in the behavioral consequences of rubella, it is not enough to discuss deafness merely in terms of sensory loss. Rather, we must concentrate on what being deaf may mean to the child and how the fact of not hearing may influence his behavior. The world of the deaf child is not merely a "world of images without sound." The congenitally deaf child has never heard sound, and the absence of this sensory dimension affects his whole way of experiencing the world. Even with the help of hearing aids, what he hears may bear little relationship to what a normal child hears because of distortions in sound. It is not strange, therefore, to read reports of deaf adolescents and adults who consider hearing people as alien to them and who find themselves much more comfortable in the presence of other deaf people. It is possible that many of the psychiatric problems called inherent to the deaf are, instead, the result of the conflict of the deaf in the hearing world. The problems may be reactive to the stress of interaction between the deaf and hearing, and not the direct consequences of sensory loss alone.

Since all deaf children function necessarily in a hearing world, even though they may attend special schools with other deaf youngsters, there are bound to be problems in their adaptation. Therefore, psychiatric problems that have frequently been itemized as characteristic of deaf children—temper tantrums, rigidity, emotional immaturity (Williams, 1970)—should be examined in terms of the basic clash between the child and the environment and not automatically as a concomitant of deafness per se.

When we consider how many of the rubella children have more than a hearing defect, it becomes obvious that it is not a simple matter to understand their behavior and to make appropriate plans for dealing with it. Even when special scales are used to test a deaf child, there are few common parameters between the investigator and the youngsters—they perform in two very different worlds. To measure intelligence is to measure adaptation against the norm of the hearing world. Basically, one is assessing how well the deaf child has adapted to the hearing world. This automatically means one is judging the child's degree and kind of communication—how does the deaf child communicate?

In the normal world, communication is primarily through language. Although it is a truism that the child who cannot hear cannot talk, these two basic capacities are usually thought of by parents of deaf children as separate entities. Lack of hearing is regarded as a physical problem which can be factually reported in terms of decibel loss or degree of severity, whereas lack of speech becomes much more tied up with lack of mental ability. This link between language and intelligence is part of our cultural heritage. Language is considered the distinctive quality of man.

Although deaf children may use gestures, pantomime, or other means of nonverbal communication, it is the fact that they don't talk that automatically sets them apart most dramatically. In the family setting, these children behave differently. Even if they have normal intelligence, they cannot ask questions about something they do not understand. The parents feel that they cannot properly carry out their role as a guiding force during this early developmental period because they are not able to inform the child and help him make new discoveries in the usual verbal way. Therefore, the parents continuously question the child's ability to move in a world where being intelligent requires the use of language. Parents of a hearing child look at linguistic mistakes as a normal part of language mastery and may not even correct the child because they know he will outgrow these errors. But the parents of a deaf child often view every error as an added barrier to even the most elementary communication and therefore invest their energies in correcting the child.

Even if the deaf child acquires language later in life, his speech may not be correct grammatically and, even more important, may be devoid of the nuances and subtleties one expects from speech. This difficulty is compounded even further when the deaf child is expected to learn to read and write.

In order to see at what level these rubella children communicated, a rough assessment of their functioning was made during the testing session.

Table 24 shows the results of this analysis of speech on the 171 children tested. As can be seen, the majority of the children had only minimal levels of communication. This is shown more clearly in Table 25 where level of speech is correlated with hearing loss.

Of the 171 children seen, 111 (64.9%) had minimal or no speech. Of these, 102 had some degree of hearing loss. The close relation between speech and hearing is indicated by the fact that 80% of those with some degree of deafness had only minimal

TABLE 24

ANALYSIS OF COMMUNICATION

Level of Communication	Number of Children
None	20
Vocalization	48
Pantomime and Gestures	42
Single Words	36
Phrases, Short or Long Sentences	60
Total*	206

* Adds up to more than the 171 tested, as some children fit into more than one category.

TABLE 25

LEVEL OF SPEECH AND HEARING LOSS

	Hearing Loss						
	Un-specified	Moderate	Severe	Profound	All Degrees	No Hearing Loss	Total
Useful Speech	3	10	5	8	26	34	60
Minimal or no Speech	6	21	41	34	102	9	111

or no speech. Of the 43 children without hearing loss, nine (20.9%) had speech difficulties. It should be recalled that these youngsters may have had other physical defects.

Although the speech defects in the deaf children may be understood in terms of a cause and effect relationship, the high incidence of speech defects in the hearing children raises further questions. Is the lack of speech in these rubella children a temporary lag or is it an additional indicator of brain dysfunction following fetal infection? An answer to this question must await follow-up studies of the children at later ages.

A large proportion of the children studied (25%) used pantomime and gestures either exclusively or in conjunction with speech in order to communicate. The whole question of their use has been raised frequently and mention should be made of some of the issues involved. Many parents reported that the special classes or clinics the child attended advised that the use of gestures should be discouraged in order to optimize the possibility of language development. Their rationale was that if a child could be understood when he gestured he would not feel the need for trying to learn the appropriate words.

It is our feeling, however, that when a child gestures or acts out he is trying to say something—he is entering into a dialogue— and all these efforts at communication should be encouraged. If the youngster is made to use a word and not allowed to gesture, there is a good chance that his curiosity about the world around him will be reduced. As a result, his capacity for formal cognitive development may be impeded. Furthermore, most profoundly deaf children cannot acquire even an elementary vocabulary until age six. If the parents insist on the exclusive use of speech at a younger age, they may reduce the youngster's motivation to learn when he is ready. Finally, it was our impression that many of the children who did use gestures had developed the most meaningful level of communication with their families. Since this degree of communication is the most crucial factor, perhaps gesturing should be accepted more in the young deaf child than it has been until now. The possibility of added difficulties in adaptation might well be minimized if the child is allowed the maximum means of expression at his command.

It is too early to say whether the rubella children's capacity to conceptualize is permanently damaged. At this point in time, however, it is obvious that for the most part they are functioning at a very low intellectual level. As compensatory operations develop, it is possible that some of them will begin to perform somewhat closer to age expectancy. But it is doubtful that the improvement will be such as to change the basically gloomy outlook for many of the youngsters.

INTERVIEW WITH THE PARENT

Having an interview with a parent, usually the mother, at the time of the psychological testing session served three major purposes:

1) It was a formal reason for the mother's presence in the room.
2) It made possible a comparison of observation of the child during the test with information given by the mother.
3) It enabled us to observe the child's behavior in relation to his mother, the examiner, and the toys in the room in an unstructured situation, since the conversation took place before testing began.

Basically, we were most interested in the parent's evaluation of a child's intelligence. We wanted to know how parents evaluated functioning in daily life and what they considered indicative of intelligence at the child's age level. A summary of the parents' estimates is given in Table 26, in terms of the categories they used for rating the children.

Of the 153 children tested and on whom the psychologist could give an estimate of intelligence, the parents of 116 also evaluated the youngsters' performance. Thirty-seven parents gave "I don't know" answers and could not be encouraged to elaborate on this. Most of these parental estimates were accurate. Ninety-one parents (78.4% of those who responded) correctly assessed their child's intellectual level. Overestimations were made by 19 parents (16.4%) and underestimations by six (5.1%).

There are several possible reasons why so many of these parents gave an accurate estimate. First, as participants in the rubella project, they were on many occasions given information on various aspects of their child's functioning. From these clues, the parents were able slowly to build up a composite picture of the youngster's level of attainment and an idea of what could be expected of him. Secondly, because of the nature of these children's handicaps, the parents had to work very closely with

TABLE 26

PARENTS' ESTIMATE OF CHILDREN'S INTELLIGENCE

Estimate	Number of Children
Bright or superior	44
Normal or average	51
Slightly below average or slow	23
Very retarded	10
No estimate	43
Total	171

them to help them master new demands. The degree of success and the amount of parental time and effort required gave an indication of the child's capacity. Also, many of the rubella youngsters had normal older siblings, and the parents no doubt compared the performances of their offspring at equivalent ages. Finally, since many of the study children attended nursery school, the parents probably received periodic evaluations from teachers against which they could compare their own impressions.

In many of the instances in which functioning was overestimated the parents appeared to equate memory of the most simple kind with intelligence. One mother was convinced that her four-year-old child was normally intelligent because he remembered that a piece of upholstery on a sofa was torn. Even after she covered the torn area with a pillow, the child kept uncovering and pointing to it. In this way, intelligent behavior appropriate for a much younger child was considered proof of adequate intellectual development at a later age. Some parents overestimated their child's intellectual level when asked directly, even though they had previously offered examples of developmental lags in many areas of functioning.

It was clear from these interviews that none of the parents viewed intellectual development as a capacity separate from other aspects of the child's emotional life. All the parents colored their estimations of intelligence with descriptions of how the child did things. They described how responsive or unresponsive the child was to their love and attention. In talking about intellectual capacity, they often referred to the emotional expectations they had and whether or not they were fulfilled. The tone of the parent-child relationship and the emotional feed-back involved in it were clearly more important to them than the particular level at which the child performed intellectually. This may be due to the young age of these children. As they grow older, intellectual capacity may become more important to the parents. But at the time of our study, emotional responsiveness rather than strict intellectual attainment was the parents' paramount concern.

7

Levels of Functioning

AN IMPORTANT ASPECT of a child's behavior is his ability to perform the various self-help activities involved in coping with the demands of daily living. We refer to this type of adaptive behavior in terms of *levels of functioning.*

Unfortunately, there are as yet no adequate measures of adaptive behavior. Existing tests, such as the Vineland Social Maturity Scale (Doll, 1953) and the Cain-Levine Social Competency Scale (Cain *et al.,* 1963), fall short as formal psychometric devices (Leland *et al.,* 1967) and also fail to describe many important aspects of an individual's effectiveness in coping with the social demands of his environment. These tests do not provide complete descriptive information about a child's capabilities in a wide range of activities, his actual competency, and the kinds of demands he encounters.

In our research with mental retardates as well as in this study of the rubella children, we realized that understanding a youngster's adaptive behavior was a vital issue in management, both in terms of his present and future performance. If too little was expected of a child, he might be handled in such a way that he could never achieve a level of functioning close to his actual capacity. Conversely, excessive expectations could impede his adaptation by producing overwhelming stress. We also realized, however, that despite the many available tests designed to estimate levels of functioning under optimal circumstances, there were no instruments specifically geared to measuring a child's actual performance in day-to-day activity. Such an estimate is vital, for it is the child's habitual level of performance that will determine his degree of success in school, in the playground, or later in a job situation. The habitual level does not necessarily correspond to the child's capability of performance under the most favorable circumstances.

The discrepancy between optimal and routine level may vary greatly from one handicapped or retarded child to another and from one activity to another. One youngster habitually functions better at home than in school; the reverse is true of another child. Such individual differences suggest that measures of capacity alone are far from adequate as predictive guides. To help a child fit into a social situation or to carry out tasks within his capacity we must know what circumstances are necessary for narrowing the gap between his capacity and actual performance.

Unless one questions parents about specific details, one may obtain quite erroneous impressions about a child's achievements. A mother may assert that her child is toilet-trained, but a pat on the youngster's rear may elicit the rustle of waterproof pants and the mother's explanation that accidents still occur with great frequency. A parent may report with full conviction that the child dresses himself completely, but inquiry into the frequency and specific circumstances discloses that his ability is not employed on school days. The reason, says the mother, is that if she is not standing by, the child tends to get garments on backwards or he dawdles interminably. The ability to dress himself completely, it turns out, is demonstrated about once a week when the child is highly motivated to get to his special recreation group on time.

We felt that the level of functioning of a rubella child was an important dimension to consider both for understanding his behavioral characteristics and for devising appropriate methods of home management. We therefore adapted the levels of functioning protocol designed originally for the study of retarded children.

LEVELS OF FUNCTIONING PROTOCOL

Information on a child's levels of functioning was obtained through a special interview with parents during which they were asked to describe the child's behavior in a specific set of activities, giving concrete examples. The parents were not just asked "Can the child dress himself?" but were questioned in detail about the skills involved in putting on clothes and the frequency with which these skills were applied. Although seven areas of activity were surveyed in the mentally retarded study, we focused on only three of them in the rubella project because 1) these were younger children and therefore could not be expected to display such activities as participation in household chores or use of money, and 2) their handicaps further limited the number of activities in which their abilities could be analyzed.

The self-help activities selected for study are universal daily activities: dressing, personal hygiene and toileting, and eating.

Dressing. Information was sought on the child's mastery of such skills as differentiating the inside and outside of a garment as well as its front and back, pulling up pants or pulling on overhead clothing, and managing fastenings such as bows, buttons, buckles, zippers, and shoelaces. These discrete skills often distinguished one child from another with respect to the ability to put on clothing without assistance. Another measure of capacity for independent performance was the youngster's recognition of the need for appropriate clothing under varying weather conditions and the increasing assumption of responsibility for the selection and care of clothing.

Personal hygiene and toileting. These activities included bathing, routine washing, care of hair, teeth, and nose, and recognition of the need for toileting, self-help in the removal of clothing, and appropriate cleansing. In all of these activities the child was rated on his ability to use bathroom and cleaning facilities and materials appropriately, for example, running water into the tub, replacing soap when finished, and flushing the toilet.

Eating. Skills related to eating included proper use of table utensils, appropriate behavior at the table (observance of customary manners), and helping one's self to food.

Within each category, questions were asked about discrete items of behavior (see Table 27). Each item was then scored in terms of both capability level and routine performance.

Capability level is defined as what the child can do without assistance. This category does not involve frequency of performance or the amount of parental supervision needed. The sole concern in scoring for capability is to determine whether a child can or cannot independently and purposefully perform the item of behavior under consideration. Five possible scores can be obtained:

1. Can do
2. Cannot do
3. No opportunity to perform
4. Never tried, although opportunity was present
5. No information (parent unable to observe the activity)

A child's capability in an area is determined by dividing the number of activities he has been observed to do at least once

TABLE 27

DISCRETE ITEMS OF BEHAVIOR INVESTIGATED IN LEVELS OF FUNCTIONING INTERVIEWS

A. *Dressing*

1. pulls up underpants
2. pulls up pajama bottoms; slacks; skirt
3. puts on open sweater; shirt; blouse; jacket; coat
4. puts on overhead clothing
5. removes underpants; slacks; skirt
6. removes open shirt; blouse
7. removes overhead clothing
8. differentiates front/back of trousers; dress; open clothing; overhead clothing
9. differentiates inside/outside of underwear; over-clothing
10. manages zipper up/down
11. engages zipper in sweater or jacket
12. unfastens large front buttons
13. unfastens small front buttons
14. fastens large front buttons
15. fastens small front buttons
16. matches button to buttonhole
17. takes off/puts on shoes; boots; rubbers; slippers
18. differentiates right/left shoes
19. laces shoes
20. ties bow
21. matches socks*
22. puts on hat; hood*
23. puts on mittens*
24. puts on gloves*
25. differentiates right/left mittens; gloves*
26. recognizes need for special clothing when it is hot; cold; raining; snowing*
27. assists in choice of daily clothing*
28. selects own clothing*
29. puts soiled clothes in designated place*
30. folds clothing*
31. hangs clothing*
32. reports tears; missing buttons*

B. *Personal Hygiene and Toileting*

1. runs water into tub and turns it off when full*
2. adjusts water temperature for washing*
3. soaps and washes self in bath
4. dries self*
5. manages routine washing of hands
6. manages routine washing of face
7. manages routine brushing or combing of hair
8. shampoos hair*
9. puts paste on toothbrush*
10. brushes own teeth*
11. rinses mouth*
12. blows nose
13. hangs up towel*
14. replaces soap in soapdish*
15. replaces toothpaste cap*
16. aware of day toileting need
17. aware of night toileting need
18. manages clothing before toileting
19. manages clothing after toileting
20. cleans self after toileting
21. flushes toilet*

C. *Eating*

1. manages cup partially filled
2. manages cup filled
3. uses spoons for all solids
4. uses spoons for liquids without spilling
5. uses fork appropriately
6. uses knife to spread butter
7. uses knife to cut soft foods
8. uses knife to cut meat
9. helps self to portions of food
10. helps self to standard items (salt, pepper, butter, etc.)
11. uses napkins*
12. helps self to drink from refrigerator*
13. removes items from table*
14. rinses used glass; dish*
15. scrapes used plates*

* Items not considered in computing % Can Do or % Does Do because very few children achieved these items or parents did not report reliably about them.

(Can Do) in a purposeful manner by the total number of skills investigated. This score reflects his "% Can Do."

Level of routine performance is broadly defined as what a child does routinely or habitually with respect to a given item of behavior. In this category it is crucial to ascertain the frequency of performance. Five scores can be obtained for each item:

1) Performs regularly, routinely
2) Performs about half the time
3) Performs sometimes
4) Performs less than half the time
5) Never performs

A child's performance score is calculated by dividing the number of items the child does do routinely by the total number of items in the behavior category. This score reflects his "% Does Do."

We also sought information on the reasons the parent helped a child when assistance was given for a specific activity. There were basically three reasons for help:

1) The child is incapable of accomplishing the activity alone
2) "Time pressures"—the child is too slow to do it alone (Help-Time)
3) The child asks for help and the parent acquiesces (Help-Asks)

We computed parental help scores only in the area of dressing. "% Help-Time" is defined as the number of skills for which the child is given help because of time pressures divided by the total number of items for which help is given. "% Help Asks" is defined as the number of skills for which the child is given help because he requests it divided by the total number of items for which help is given.

To insure that all three activity areas would be covered, a detailed interview guide was printed. Furthermore, the interviewers were instructed that to meet scoring criteria, statements had to be descriptive of specific self-help skills. Generalized statements and evaluative ratings, such as are usually found in parental reports, were rejected unless buttressed by an objective detailed description of an event. This requirement guards against the presumptive nature of the data in many conventional tests of social competency.

The scoring system for the levels of functioning data was applied to each discrete aspect of behavior enumerated on our check list. That is, for each item—manages cup filled, blows nose, fastens large buttons—a score was assigned for capability level and frequency of successful performance. From the array of item scores, the general scores (% Can Do, % Does Do) were derived to characterize each child's pattern of functioning.

LEVELS OF FUNCTIONING IN RUBELLA CHILDREN

It was not possible to assess the level of functioning of each of the 243 children in the behavioral study for two reasons. First, nine youngsters in the sample were institutionalized and data on their adaptive behavior could not be obtained. Secondly, because of their handicaps, 81 other youngsters were not capable of performing even a minimum number (at least one) of the self-help skills we surveyed. Thus, there were at most 153 children capable of some self-help activities. The data discussed below accurately describe the level of functioning of those youngsters with at least some degree of self-help capability, though they overestimate the achievements of the sample as a whole.

Table 28 lists the mean (and median) capability and performance scales of the children who could be scored. The most striking feature of these data is the marked discrepancy between what the children are capable of doing and what they routinely perform.

In the area of dressing, the mean % Can Do score was 74.0 with an S.D. of 20.0. The median score was 79.7 and indicates that half the children on whom information could be obtained

TABLE 28

LEVELS OF FUNCTIONING SCORES OF CHILDREN CAPABLE OF SOME SELF-HELP ACTIVITIES

	Dressing		Eating		Personal Hygiene & Toileting	
	% Can Do	% Does Do	% Can Do	% Does Do	% Can Do	% Does Do
N	153	136	153	112	150	105
Mean	74.0	31.3	65.9	32.4	85.1	53.5
Standard Deviation	20.0	28.2	20.1	25.2	19.3	27.8
Median	79.7	22.8	69.9	27.0	92.1	57.8

can do at least 80% of the activities necessary to dress themselves. However, the median score for % Does Do is only 22.8%, indicating that fewer than half of the children do as much as 25 per cent of the self-help skills necessary for dressing. Looking at these data from a somewhat different angle, it can be seen that based on the average scores the youngsters do less than half (42.3%) of what they are able to do.

Similarly, in the area of eating, the children on the average can do 65.9% of the specific tasks involved, but they routinely perform only 32.4% of these items, or approximately half of their known capability.

With regard to personal hygiene and toileting activities, the same trend persists, although there is a slightly smaller discrepancy between the children's capacity and performance. Thus, the children can do an average of 85.1% of the activities involved, while they actually and habitually accomplish somewhat more than half of them. In terms of capability, they perform routinely at almost two-thirds of capacity. It is possible that performance in this area is the highest because of the specific nature of the activities involved or because the range of skills required is the simplest of the three areas investigated.

For the most part gross motor coordination is required, rather than the fine motor abilities needed to button buttons and tie shoelaces. In addition, this is an area in which parental concern

TABLE 29

Frequency Distribution of Levels of Functioning Scores

% Score	Dressing Can Do No. Children	Dressing Does Do No. Children	Eating Can Do No. Children	Eating Does Do No. Children	Personal Hygiene & Toileting Can Do No. Children	Personal Hygiene & Toileting Does Do No. Children
90-100	47	11	14	6	101	12
80-89	30	4	26	2	22	8
70-79	28	4	38	3	4	11
60-69	14	2	29	5	7	19
50-59	13	12	18	8	4	15
40-49	11	8	6	14	6	10
30-39	5	9	13	14	2	6
20-29	3	24	4	16	2	7
10-19	2	26	5	21	0	5
0- 9	0	36	0	23	2	12
Total No. of Children	153	136	153	112	150	105

is quite prominent. All the parents were most anxious that their children become toilet-trained. This developmental milestone was as important to them as it is to all other parents. We may speculate that they were less willing to continue servicing the youngsters in this area and worked especially hard at getting them to become self-reliant. This parental encouragement may be responsible for the increased performance scores in this area and for the decreased discrepancy between what the children on the whole could and did do.

Although the two scores, capability and performance, measure two independently defined aspects of a child's adaptive behavior, the question remains whether the two scores are so related to one another that they are functionally redundant. To answer this, it was helpful to look at the frequency distribution of individual % Can Do and % Does Do scores (see Table 29).

It can be seen from Table 29 that of the 47 children capable of 90 to 100 per cent of the dressing items, only 11 routinely performed up to capacity. The majority routinely did less than what they could do and are included in the figures for lower Does Do scores. Similarly, although 36 children habitually executed 0 to 9 per cent of the dressing items, all of them had at least about 10% more capability than they routinely displayed.

These figures indicate that those children who were most capable of tasks, as reported by their parents, were not necessarily those who most regularly did the things they were able to do. This confirms the suggestion that capability and performance be considered separate aspects of a child's level of functioning.

Comparisons with Mentally Retarded Study Children

Similar discrepancies between capability and routine performance were found in the study of mentally retarded children described earlier. Despite their older age, the average % Can Do score for the retarded study youngsters was 74.6 for a broad range of self-help skills that included those surveyed for the rubella children. Of the items reported that the children Can Do, the median Does Do score was 72.5%. Thus, half the children could be counted on routinely to perform about three-quarters of what they were reported to be actually capable of doing. In general, it was found that almost one-third of the children had a marked discrepancy between their level of capability and their level of actual performance. Furthermore, the routine level of functioning was not simply related to the more conventional measures, such as IQ, MA, or CA; no significant correlations were found between them.

PARENTAL HELP

In the area of dressing, we analyzed the number of times the child received help from a parent either because he did not act quickly enough to meet the pressures of time or because he requested aid. The frequency distributions of the % Help-Time and % Help-Ask scores are shown in Table 30, and the average scores for the sample surveyed are given in Table 31.

TABLE 30

FREQUENCY DISTRIBUTION OF % HELP SCORES IN THE AREA OF DRESSING

	Help Given Because of Time Pressure % Help-Time (No. of Children)	Help Given Because of Child's Request % Help-Ask (No. of Children)
90-100	10	0
80-89	0	0
70-79	3	0
60-69	5	0
50-59	18	2
40-49	11	5
30-39	21	9
20-29	25	8
10-19	16	21
0-9	17	79
Total No. of Children	126	124

TABLE 31

AVERAGE DRESSING HELP SCORES FOR THE GROUP

	Help-Time (N=126)	Help-Ask (N=124)
Mean	36.6%	12.1%
S.D.	24.9%	12.5%
Median	31.9%	7.8%

This analysis reveals a general tendency for the parents to help a child despite the fact that he was capable of independent performance. Thus, an average of 12 per cent of the help given the children in getting dressed was in response to their requests for assistance and three times as much help (36.6%) was provided because of time pressures. Again, these findings parallel those of the retarded study in which the parents also serviced children in areas in which they were able to perform independently.

TABLE 32

MEAN % DOES DO SCORES OF CHILDREN WITH DIFFERENT NUMBERS OF DEFECTS

Number of Defect Areas	Dressing		Eating		Personal Hygiene & Toileting	
	Mean % Does Do	S.D.	Mean % Does Do	S.D.	Mean % Does Do	S.D.
0	42.2	35.1	32.1	27.5	64.7	26.4
1	30.0	31.2	37.5	32.7	56.2	30.2
2	36.8	33.0	23.3	21.2	46.1	32.9
3	19.0	27.2	25.3	16.0	36.4	29.2
4	9.2	8.0	35.0	45.1	41.7	24.8

Quite commonly the parents said it was so much easier for them to dress the child than to let him perform alone that they took action even when it wasn't necessary. They also noted that since the children had so many things to do they wanted to help whenever they could, and this was an easy area in which they could assist. Tied in with this was their desire, whenever possible, to make things as easy as they could for their handicapped child. While time pressures, in some instances, made their help mandatory—the child had to be ready for the nursery school bus promptly—on other occasions time pressures were used as an excuse to allay their discomfort at seeing a youngster struggle on his own to get dressed. However, what the parents often did not realize was that by continuing to service the youngster they were preventing him from optimizing his self-reliance.

LEVELS OF FUNCTIONING AND PHYSICAL DEFECTS

Obviously, what a child *can* do is directly related to his physical condition. The relationship between what he does routinely and his areas of physical competence is somewhat less clear-cut, but one would expect that children with fewer defects would be more likely to accomplish a higher proportion of the necessary self-help skills than their more handicapped peers. This appeared to be the case.

TABLE 33

% DOES DO SELF-HELP IN CHILDREN WITH DIFFERENT
AREAS OF DEFECT

Defect Area	Dressing		Eating		Personal Hygiene & Toileting	
	Mean % Does Do	S.D.	Mean % Does Do	S.D.	Mean % Does Do	S.D.
Hearing	26.9	30.3	29.8	28.5	47.0	30.9
Vision	23.2	30.0	29.4	24.8	45.2	31.0
Neurolog- ical (Hard)	13.2	17.0	23.8	22.5	34.8	29.8
Neurolog- ical (Soft)	25.3	30.4	20.7	23.0	37.9	32.2
Cardiac	21.0	27.4	26.8	22.9	41.9	21.6

As Table 32 highlights, children with three or four defects on the average perform less than 20% of the dressing items surveyed and only about 35 to 40% of the personal hygiene and toileting activities. Those with two or fewer defects perform proportionately more of the necessary self-help items. In the area of eating, the relationship between the number of defects a child has and how much he does for himself is not meaningful. This may be due to the fact that parents can be more flexible in accommodating a child's handicaps or preferences in this area.

The data in Table 33 make it apparent that, on the average, children with hearing defects have the highest relative self-help scores even though they are far from routinely performing even half of the activities subsumed in each of the three areas. This may be due to the nature of the defect as well as the fact that hearing defects occurred in isolation more frequently than the other handicaps. Children with hard neurological signs routinely performed much less often in the areas of dressing and toileting than youngsters with other defects, and those with hard and soft signs had the lowest scores in the area of eating.

Another way of looking at the relationship between defect area and level of functioning is presented in Table 34 where

TABLE 34

AVERAGE % OF WHAT THE CHILDREN CAN DO THAT IS ROUTINELY PERFORMED

Defect Area	Dressing	Eating	Personal Hygiene & Toileting
Hearing	63	51	42
Vision	63	49	40
Neurological (Hard)	78	55	50
Neurological (Soft)	57	57	43
Cardiac	68	48	44

the focus is on the percentage of what a child can do that he routinely does rather than on the percentage of *all* items that he can be counted on to do.

The scores summarized in Table 34 reflect the actualization of the children's self-help skills—that part of what they can do that they in fact displayed. These scores do not reflect true self-help ability, since a child with few skills who performs all of them will score 100%, while a child with many skills who routinely accomplishes only half will score 50%. It should be remembered, therefore, that the lower scores do not mean less capability *per se*. Rather, they indicate that the child merely *does* less than he is capable of doing.

From these data, there does not appear to be a consistent relationship between type of defect and the degree to which the children routinely do that of which they are capable. Children with hard neurological signs, however, do seem routinely to perform closer to their capacities than children with other defects, particularly in terms of dressing and toileting, even though they habitually do only half to three-quarters of what they are able to do. It should be recalled, however, that children with hard neurological signs habitually carry out fewer self-help skills than children with other defects even though they are routinely doing a larger percentage of the activities they actually can do.

Although these data indicate a large discrepancy between capability and performance, they do not tell us *why* the discrepancy exists. Nevertheless, it is likely that the degree to which a child routinely does that of which he is capable depends on his temperamental characteristics and the way in which he is handled by his parents. The lack of independent functioning in these children must be considered in planning management and training programs for them.

DISCUSSION

Various studies of the cognitive functioning of children have shown that "performance levels under particular conditions are but fragmentary indicators of capacity" (Bortner and Birch, 1970). The acceptance of this distinction is confirmed by the concentrated attention given to children considered "underachievers" at school.

In the area of adaptive behavior, the same distinction between capacity and performance also pertains. As any mother of a school age child (who has had to replace a toothpaste cap, hang up a towel, and rinse out the sink after the morning rush is over) can relate, there is often a vast difference between what her son or daughter can do and what he routinely does. This discrepancy is highlighted at various stages of a child's development.

In the normal child without physical or intellectual defects, the discrepancy may be a source of complaint, but it rarely is a cause of concern. Once a normal child has shown a capacity to act in a certain area, there is justifiable assurance that he will in time routinely perform the behavioral item without the parents hovering over him. Even if a parent takes over and helps the child in an area in which the youngster is capable of performance but moves too slowly, this overservicing will eventually cease when normal development and the stimulus of peer pressures converge to facilitate independent action. Thus, the parent who completes the job of shoelace tying for a five-year-old who is rushing to get out of the house need not worry that the child will never tie his own laces. Within a short time, his physical coordination will have matured enough so that he can do it quickly, and the need to service himself at school will motivate him to perform routinely. In short, capacity-performance discrepancies do not usually play a crucial role in normal adaptive development so long as parental expectations and demands remain consonant with the child's organismic characteristics.

With regard to the handicapped youngster, however, these discrepancies acquire new significance. In the first place, parents do not always know what to expect of their physically or intellectually handicapped child. The surrounding environment, peopled with normally developing youngsters, provides few if any guidelines for assessing the stages of development of the child with defects. Parents must be helped to determine just what their child is and should be capable of doing at each age.

Secondly, it cannot be assumed that because the child is competent in some skill he will incorporate it into his repertoire of routine activities. In many cases, the parents of a handicapped child substitute estimates of capability for estimates of competence. For example, if asked, *"Does he cut his food with a knife?"* they will answer, "He *can*," and further questioning is required to reveal that the youngster eats only soft or finger foods that are easily managed. By focusing on capability rather than performance, the parents thus deny the actual limitations in the child's performance and, as a result, overlook the need for training. Similarly, by frequently helping a competent child because of "time pressures," they fail to optimize his performance.

Extrafamilial factors also play a part. Very often the handicapped child will be isolated to a greater or lesser degree from normal peers and therefore lack the stimulation of their performance to encourage his own. And, even if he is in close contact with nonhandicapped children, knowing that he is different from them in some areas may prevent him from attempting to do even those of their activities of which he is capable—he just assumes he can't perform, so doesn't.

Additionally, there is the tendency when training handicapped children, to use rote methods in an optimum environment. Thus, the youngster learns basic steps necessary to complete a task within a protective home setting. When he then moves into a new milieu, away from the supporting parent and geographical location, it is not unusual to find his performance deteriorated. This tendency toward "fixed" functioning is further compounded by the absence of built-in methods of self-correction. While the normal youngster, therefore, often will perform better away from home, the handicapped child usually does worse. Even if he has the capacity to act, he may not "rise to the occasion" because the exact circumstances in which he has adapted are different.

This means that increased emphasis must be placed on the *routine* performance of the child with defects. For him, each iota of competence is likely to make a great difference in his ability to be incorporated in a learning, recreational, or social situation. One cannot assume he will eventually come to do that of which he is capable on his own. Rather, this actualization must be encouraged consistently. In order for him to achieve any measure of success, he *must* come to do most of what he is capable in a routine fashion—and this achievement cannot be left to time alone. His caretakers must realistically estimate his capacities and do all they can to realize his potential.

It is in this perspective that the discrepancy between capacity and performance is most profitably viewed. This is not a way of distinguishing normal from handicapped children, but of calling attention to the need for outside intervention to bridge the gap in the handicapped. While no individual can function at full capacity all the time, the degree to which a child with defects falls below his maximum ability may be crucial. For it may determine whether he can take part in normal life or must lead a protected existence.

8

Behavioral Assessment of Children with Neurological Defects

MANY OF THE RUBELLA CHILDREN had neurological defects ranging from soft signs, such as clumsiness, to hard signs, such as spasticity and other severe neuromuscular handicaps usually subsumed in the diagnosis of cerebral palsy. Generally, such physical signs are taken as presumptive evidence of central nervous system dysfunction. Since rubella virus has been isolated from brain tissue and cerebrospinal fluid of fetally-infected children at autopsy as well as during the first 18 months of life, we had to consider the possibility of brain damage as the etiological factor. We were especially interested in determining if there were any behavior patterns specifically characteristic of rubella children with neurological defects (and possibly some degree of cerebral dysfunction) that would warrant considering them separately from the other damaged youngsters.

Earlier observations of children who had suffered known cerebral insults led to the description of the "hyperkinetic" syndrome. Strauss and Werner (1941) were the first to delineate the behavioral sequelae of minimal central nervous system damage in children. These investigators included as "brain damaged" those youngsters who were hyperactive, emotionally labile, perceptually disordered, impulsive, and distractible. Their findings led to an unfortunate syllogism, however: children with known brain damage exhibit, or may exhibit, such and such behavior; the patient under study displays similar behavior; ergo, he is brain damaged. Thus there has been a persistent tendency to refer to all minimally brain-damaged children as a unitary group characterized as hyperkinetic and to diagnose any hyperkinetic child as brain-damaged, often through circular reasoning.

The common assumption of an organically-determined "hyperkinetic" syndrome has been challenged, and the behaviors displayed by children with cerebral dysfunction are now thought to be extremely varied. There is a paucity of evidence that children who exhibit the Straussian pattern do in fact have brain damage (Birch, 1964). Conversely, many children with organic damage that has been verified through neurologic or anatomic examination do not exhibit the patterns of behavior presumed to be characteristic of "brain damage." While hyperkinesis frequently comes to clinical notice, it is neither synonymous with nor pathognomonic for brain damage. In addition, even when a child has obvious brain damage and also displays the classical signs of hyperkinesis, one cannot prove a causal relationship between them; the two findings can merely be said to be concurrent.

Obviously, in some cases, a causal relationship between cerebral dysfunction and behavioral items will be somewhat more readily recognized. When a child has a degenerative disease of the brain, his loss of interest in his surroundings and his lowered intellectual functioning may be understood as direct symptoms of the organic changes. In the epileptic child, irritability in personality makeup may be a direct result of brain irritation. Similarly, when brain tissue is destroyed by an injury or a tumor, functioning formerly controlled by the affected portion of the brain may be disrupted.

A brain lesion, however, does not necessarily lead to behavioral disturbances. Even when hard neurological signs are present, one cannot automatically conclude that a specific behavioral pattern will follow in the wake of the presumed brain damage. Many brain-damaged children are able to make a healthy adjustment to their circumstances, and the only distortions may be in their motor activity.

Several surveys have found a wide variety of behavioral patterns in children who have neurological defects that may stem from cerebral dysfunction. As Pond (1961) reported in his review of hospitalized children, "the symptoms are extraordinarily varied, and it is clear at once that the classical syndrome of the brain-damaged child does not cover more than a few of the children seen."

It is possible that this reported diversity of behavior in part reflects the heterogeneous grouping in some studies of children with vastly different neurological signs. In view of this possibility, we thought it practical in our study to isolate the data on those children with gross evidence of cerebral palsy in order to see if in this restricted group a specific behavioral pattern would be found concurrent with neuromotor defects (see Table 35).

Of the 33 children diagnosed as cerebral palsied by the neurologists at the RBDEP, 7 (21.2%) had no psychiatric disorder and functioned at a normal intellectual level. One child had a reactive behavior disorder but was of normal intelligence. The remaining 25 youngsters, 75.8% of this subsample, were retarded to a degree ranging from mild to profound. Retardation was the sole psychiatric finding in 20 children in this group. The other 5 youngsters displayed disordered behavior in addition to their intellectual retardation.

These figures highlight the difficulty one encounters in trying to understand the behavior of brain-damaged children. They re-

TABLE 35

PSYCHIATRIC FINDINGS IN CEREBRAL PALSIED CHILDREN
(includes four at Willowbrook)

Diagnosis	No. of Children
No Disorder	7
Reactive Behavior Disorder	1
Mental Retardation—mild	2
moderate	5
severe	8
profound	5
Mental Retardation + Behavior Disorder	5
Total	33

veal the fallacy of assuming that there is such a thing as "the brain damage behavioral syndrome." Here we have a separate group of cerebral palsied children in whom some degree of cerebral dysfunction exists. And even in this group, we find that brain damage does not necessarily yield behavior disorder and that even when there is a concurrent behavior disorder the symptoms do not necessarily reflect the often-described syndrome.

The children in this sample ranged from those who were functioning in a completely age-appropriate fashion to those who were intellectually retarded and also had severe behavior problems. The most common finding was mental retardation, and although this impairment might be directly related to brain damage, the fact that eight youngsters performed at least at an average level emphasizes the well known fact that cerebral dysfunction does not necessarily affect intelligence.

CHILDREN WITH BEHAVIOR DISORDERS

When we look at those children who had behavior disorders, we find even here a wide range of presenting problems. One non-retarded child had a reactive disorder. Both his parents were drug addicts, hospitalized for detoxification. The child lived with his maternal grandmother who handled him in an inconsistent, overpermissive fashion. The child's teasing and moderately undisciplined behavior was considered to be in direct response to this care.

The other five children with behavior disorders were also mentally retarded. Their behavioral difficulties ranged from reactive responses to extremely serious deviances in affective behavior with autistic features.

One of these children, Marie, was considered to have a reactive behavior disorder and to be mildly retarded. In addition to spastic quadriparesis, she has congenital heart disease, mild visual loss, and a profound hearing loss. Marie gets angry easily and proceeds to scream, stamp her feet, and cry. These temper tantrums are usually in response to parental demands for immediate compliance with their orders for undressing or going to bed. In other circumstances, however, her behavior is appropriate.

In contrast to Marie, whose behavior disorder is really rather mild, is Karen, a moderately deaf youngster with spastic quadriparesis and congenital heart disease. She is a severely retarded child whose behavior has definite autistic features. During most of the psychiatric interview, Karen sat and sucked her thumb, or else rocked back and forth. She displayed no meaningful interaction with her mother. She cried and smiled to herself, and no attempts at obtaining an affective response were successful. Similarly, during the psychological test session she showed no affective responses, and the mother had to turn the child's head toward her when she wanted Karen's attention. At home, too, even when her brothers are in the room with her talking and playing, she has no interaction with them. She usually just "rolls about a lot from side to side on her back." Neither her physical handicaps nor her retardation appears sufficient to explain these definitely autistic features in her behavior.

In between these extremes were three children with a variety of symptoms. One young girl, Marcia, in addition to being cerebral palsied had a severe to profound hearing loss and congenital heart disease. She was severely retarded in her growth; at age five years three months she weighed only 29 pounds. Behaviorally, although she is an "affectionate" child according to her mother, she has tantrums easily when made to do something she does not want to do. For example, if she's told to move from a chair, she throws herself down on the floor, screams, and kicks. Her mother says that disciplining Marcia is her largest problem.

Norma, another cerebral palsied child with severe hearing loss and congenital heart disease, was characterized behaviorally by her hyperactivity. She frequently hit other children "in an uncontrollable way" and appeared "angry almost all the time." Her mother described her as "a very violent child." In addition, "she is not afraid of anything, not even fire. She has burned herself several times but always goes back to the stove. She runs in front of cars in the street and sometimes sits in the middle of the street when a car is coming."

Kathy was moderately to severely deaf and cerebral palsied. She was hyperactive and perseverative. Furthermore, she tended to put every object she found into her mouth. The mother said she had to "strip the house so she can't swallow small objects. She chews (and swallows) soap, perfume, deodorant." She also bangs her head against chairs and grinds her teeth. Her hyperactivity was characterized by rapid movements and frantic touching of objects, none of which she explored in a purposeful way. Although she has been making a fair amount of progress in a rehabilitative program since she was evaluated by us, she remains hyperactive and her attention span is most unpredictable. She also has developed a seizure disorder.

From this discussion, it is obvious that merely knowing a child is brain-damaged does not tell us anything about what his behavior will be like. One may expect that he will be mentally retarded, but even this is not always the case.

Our findings are limited to symptoms observed when these rubella children were of preschool age. As they get older, the incidence of behavior disorders other than mental retardation may very well increase. In the first place, it is possible that when schooling begins various cognitive disabilities related to brain dysfunction may become apparent. These do not necessarily arise *de novo* at school age but will only be elicited by the academic demands made of these children. For example, a child whose language is now considered up to age and whose vocabulary is excellent may become unable to integrate his communicative capabilities when this is necessary. He might become "frozen" at this stage of his development and later evaluations will show below-age functioning or an aphasic disorder. This frequently has been seen to happen with brain-damaged children. Similarly, when time becomes a parameter in determining a child's performance due to the exigencies of school life, perseveration may become apparent. The young child who sticks with an activity for long periods of time may not be considered unusual, since it frequently is convenient to his parents for him to be so occupied. However, in school, when he must be able to change from one activity to another at his teacher's request, this stick-to-it-iveness may, for the first time, be evaluated as the perseveration it really is. Another capacity that might be affected by brain damage is memory, and this faculty too cannot be fully assessed until the child faces specific learning demands that require him to organize and recapture previously assimilated pieces of knowledge. Only at such a time will it become obvious if the child is or is not able to perform up to age expectancy.

In addition to these discrete areas of performance that may have a direct relationship to brain damage and which may become problem areas as the children grow older, there are various affective disorders that may develop as these physically handicapped youngsters are exposed to more and more of a world of normal people from whom they realize they differ. Thus, various symptoms such as avoidance, clowning, negativism, and withdrawal may extend the brain-damaged child's handicap beyond the area of the primary defect. A child who has difficulty in concentration or coordination may assume a passive, dependent role, letting others do his thinking and acting. He may come to feel that he cannot carry out tasks or take care of himself. A child with uncontrollable muscular impulses that make writing difficult may refuse to use the special pencil devised to minimize his difficulty, and he may have a temper tantrum whenever attention is focused on his weakness. Brain-damaged children who continually experience partial failure because of their handicap may tend to freeze into silence, or they may show overt symptoms of anxiety.

Obviously, whether these affective problems develop depends upon both the child's personality makeup and the way in which he is handled by his parents. Thus, although Marie was the most severely damaged child in physical terms, she had one of the mildest behavior disorders. Temperamentally, she approached new experiences and was usually of positive mood. Handling by the parents was for the most part permissive, perhaps because of their concern for the child's health. They were inconsistent in their demands of her, because they did not know if she could even understand them. As a result, they sometimes forced issues which at other times they let pass. Therefore the child's tantrum reactions were usually evoked in situations where she had no clear guide to her parents' expectations.

This review of the behavioral characteristics of the rubella children who could be presumed to be brain-damaged points out the need to attend carefully to the individual ways in which this deviance will become apparent. Any remediation of these handicapped children will have to weigh carefully each factor involved, including neurological insult.

9

The Autistic Rubella Child

SPECIFIC REFERENCES TO AUTISM in rubella children were fragmentary before the 1964 epidemic. For example, Rimland (1964)
mentions one case treated in the Netherlands by Dr. Arn. Van
Krevelen. Recent studies, however, clearly suggest that autistic
behavior is one of the possibilities to which the clinician must be
alerted in dealing with rubella children.

In the Baylor University series, of the 64 children surviving
at 18 months of age, eight "appeared autistic, isolated and out
of communication with the environment" (Desmond et al., 1970).
Another report (Freedman et al., 1970) describes in detail one
multihandicapped rubella baby for whom the diagnosis of infantile autism appeared appropriate to the authors.

In our own study, we have found a much higher prevalence

113

of behavioral disturbances than one would normally expect. This has been particularly striking with regard to autism. We identified ten youngsters as autistic in their total behavioral adaptation. These children presented a picture of autism corresponding in most respects to Kanner's classical criteria for infantile autism. An additional eight children showed a significant number of signs of autistic behavior. In these cases, the term "partial syndrome of autism" was employed.

These prevalence figures are obviously very high when compared with the expectancy of autism in the general population. In one British survey, a total of 4.5 per 10,000 children were found to be autistic (Lotter, 1966); another British study reported 4 cases in 9,000 schoolchildren (Rutter, 1966); a recent American survey classified a total of 3.1 per 10,000 children as having childhood schizophrenia, including autism (Treffert, 1970). By contrast, the prevalence rate in our sample of rubella children corresponds to 412 per 10,000 for the core syndrome of autism and 329 per 10,000 for the partial syndrome, yielding a combined figure of 741 per 10,000.

Of the ten autistic children we studied, nine also had varying degrees of retardation: one youngster was intellectually normal. Of the eight children with partial syndrome of autism, only one was not retarded. One of the remainder had additional symptoms of cerebral dysfunction.

Since these figures suggest the possibility that autism has been confused with mental retardation—a not uncommon occurrence—it is appropriate to note that a recent study of 52 retarded children (Chess and Hassibi, 1970) did not yield a single case of autism. Indeed, a major conclusion of this study was a warning against the assumption that certain behavioral expressions in retarded children, such as stereotypy and repetitiveness, are necessarily signs of autism.

The major criteria for our diagnosis of autism derive from Kanner's classical description of children with disturbances of affective contact. Kanner (1943) delineated a group of children who from birth gave little evidence of ability to relate to people. Their verbal utterances were monotonously repetitive and did not convey meaning to others, though the children had good rote memory. They displayed an obsessive desire for maintaining sameness. While their capacity for spontaneous activity was limited, they could relate to objects and play happily with them for hours. Among other characteristic behaviors was the failure of such youngsters to look directly at people: they gazed to the side or focused beyond; they did not make visual contact with the eyes of the individual attempting to gain their attention. (The youngsters described by Kanner did not have sensory defect, their intelligence levels were generally normal, and there were no significant neurological findings.)

In the three decades since Kanner's original paper, concepts of autism have proliferated. The main trends are conveniently reviewed by Rutter (1968). Various investigators have pursued Kanner's description in different directions. Some have advanced a psychogenic hypothesis, and others have focused on organic etiology. Some view autism as a variety of mental subnormality, whereas others claim that autistic children are basically of normal intelligence. The research returns are not all in; therefore, nobody can claim a monopoly of insight. But the basic behavioral features depicted by Kanner have stood the test of time, especially the "extreme autistic aloneness," language abnormalities, stereotypic relations to the environment. The lack of affective human contact remains the primary sign.

SENSORY DEFECTS AND AFFECTIVE BEHAVIOR

Since our sample included so many children who were retarded and had multiple sensory disabilities, we had to be particularly careful to differentiate between children whose "aloneness" directly reflected these handicaps and those whose affective contact was inherently disturbed. One cannot judge by peculiar mannerisms or ritualistic behavior, since these may be exhibited by children who are simply retarded and by both autistic and nonautistic children with sensory lack. Generally it is assumed that mannerisms causing excitation of nerve endings, such as the photic stimulation of eyeball pressing or the vestibular stimulation of head shaking and of lying with head down, do not necessarily represent an actual preference for nonhuman over human relatedness. Given a choice, our nonautistic children prefer people to things.

It may be argued that the isolating effect of living in a world with muted light and muted or absent sound can play a part in creating interpersonal distance. Whether this is to be considered stress is unclear. Experimental deprivation of sensory experience in sensorially normal individuals has been stressful to the point of creating hallucinations. This finding, however, cannot be mechanically applied to our rubella children. The issue here is not that of going from a world of stimuli to one deprived of sight and sound, but of having from birth experienced fewer stimuli than the child with normal visual or auditory function. Where visual remediation (cataract removal plus glasses) or auditory support (hearing aids) has been provided, one notes a dramatic contrast in reports on autistic and nonautistic children. The latter, after a period of getting used to the devices, respond by spontaneously putting on glasses and hearing aids on arising in the morning, and removing them only on going to bed. When a battery wears out in a hearing aid, the child removes the device during the day, and this is often the first signal a parent has that the hearing aid isn't working. The autistic child, however, does not respond in this fashion. With him it is particularly difficult to test the degree of hearing impairment and to determine to what degree remediation is effective.

Another significant difference between the autistic and nonautistic rubella children with sensory defects is the use they make of alternative, relatively intact modes of experiencing. Nonautistic youngsters whose only sensory lack is hearing are very alert to their surroundings through their other senses, especially ex-

TABLE 36

COMPARISON OF DEFECTS WITH AFFECTIVE DISORDERS

Defect	Autism	Partial Autism	No affective disorder
Visual only	0	0	4
Hearing only	0	1	83
Retardation only	0	0	4
Visual + hearing	1	0	12
Visual + retardation	0	0	6
Hearing + retardation	4	3	19
Hearing + visual + retardation	5	4	45

hibiting visual alertness and appropriate responsiveness. Children with multiple handicaps may also be markedly responsive, not only through residual sensory capacities, but also through seeking of affectionate bodily contact. Some are shy, some slow to warm up, some perhaps wary; but one is impressed by their readiness to respond to appropriately selected and carefully timed overtures. In contrast, the autistic children neither explore alternative sensory modalities nor manifest appropriate responsiveness. They form a distinct group whose distance from people cannot be adequately explained by the degree or combination of visual and auditory loss, nor by the degree of retardation where this also exists. Moreover, whether retarded or not, their affective behaviors do not resemble those of children of their obtained mental age— in fact, there is no mental age for which the behaviors are appropriate.

The presence of sensory and cognitive defect does not in itself account for the number of rubella children who fulfill the criteria for autism. As Table 36 shows, children with similar defects, whether single or multiple, may or may not have an affective disorder. Nor does the degree of defect necessarily determine the affective contact achieved by the children. A severely retarded 3-year-old with severe hearing impairment may gurgle and kick in pleased response to being tickled. Yet a mildly retarded autistic

3-year-old with moderate hearing loss may endlessly manipulate the pieces of a puzzle, but acknowledge the presence of people only by poking at their eyes with a toy.

COMMUNICATION

In the area of communication, also, the autistic children were different. In our study the autistic youngsters differed basically from the other sensorially impaired children in that they did not have a repertoire of gestures: they did not point; they did not pantomime; they were often absorbed in activities such as hand and head movements, sucking fingers, sucking clothes, and walking in circles.

Other rubella children with profound hearing loss also could not speak, but were able to communicate through gestures. They acted out, they pointed, they entered into a meaningful dialogue. Quite often they were extremely persistent about making sure that the other person had really understood what they wanted to express. Their whole body seemed to expect tensely the right sign or action from the listener that would indicate comprehension; if they had doubts, they often repeated their gestures spontaneously.

Whereas parents of the autistic children talked about their child's inability to respond affectively—they often qualified their kisses as "mechanical"—the parents of nonautistic sensorially damaged youngsters said that, although the children could not talk, they were very affectionate and they and the parents derived mutual joy from this affection. Many of these children showed through meaningful actions their awareness of parents' likes and dislikes. Their level of sensitivity and compassion was often considered finer than that of older siblings.

The following two vignettes from psychiatric interviews are typical of rubella children judged to be autistic.

Steven is 5 years, 8 months. Physically he appears to be his stated age. He has a cataract in his left eye plus right eye

rubella retinopathy. There is some question about the presence and degree of hearing loss. He functions at borderline
intelligence. Steven did not respond to verbal or physical
overtures by the examiner and had to be carried into the
playroom by the psychologist, who had completed a testing
session with him shortly before. The boy gave no sign of
recognition or response to the psychologist, nor to his father,
with whom he had been walking about in the other room.
In the playroom Steven spontaneously reached for the nameplate pinned to the examiner's coat. When the examiner
removed the nameplate and held it behind her, then dropped
it into her pocket, Steven sought it in both places. He
seemed unaware of the examiner and did not look directly at
her. He then removed the toy cooking utensils from a com-
partment of the toy cabinet, placed them in the next com-
partment, and attempted to climb into the cubby hole. His
motor control was good.

Carried repeatedly to the play table, he finally attended
to the form board, and quickly placed the 10 pieces in their
recessed spaces. Although he made errors with several of the
pieces, these were errors for which there was some basis—
he tried to put a star into a triangular recess, a rectangle
into a square—and he quickly corrected the error. The
child then returned to his attempt to get the nameplate,
looking first at its original position, then seeking it in the
pocket where he had last seen it. At no time did he utter
a word or sound, nor did he respond to his name or any
verbal direction.

Mark is a healthy looking, chubby boy who appears
to be of appropriate size for his age of 4 years, 8 months. He
has severe deafness and bilateral retinopathy and functions
on a severely retarded level. His parents have described his
ritualistic behavior and failure to communicate either by
speech or gesture. He was first seen in the playroom, where
he had run directly on entering the examiner's office. His
mother explained that he had seen the psychologist there and
had apparently remembered the blocks. When the examiner
walked into the playroom, Mark was engrossed with bringing
one block into position with another. He made almost continuous noises with his tongue protruding between his lips,

producing a sound like an unending "Bronx cheer." When called loudly, he made no response. When his arm and leg were patted, he made no response. The examiner tried to lift Mark's bowed head by placing a hand under his chin, but the child resisted and would not look up. Mark paid no attention when a fire truck was put in front of him, but when the examiner reached down with a duck puppet, the boy immediately put his hand in the duck's beak for a fleeting moment. During the period of observation, when left alone, Mark did nothing but repetitively oppose the end of one block to the end of another. All this time he continued to make the noise with his lips and tongue. There was no change in facial expression.

FAMILY STRESS

It was of interest to examine the autistic rubella child in relation to his family, both in terms of his impact on their style of life and the attitudes they displayed toward him. In our study group, proportionately more children with autism caused family stress than did those without autism. An autistic child was more likely to alter the family's mode of life and affect their approach to training. Overpermissiveness was the most pronounced characteristic of parental handling. At this stage we can only offer data correlations, without attempting a conclusive judgment as to which factors were causative and which were derivative. Our conjecture is that the contrasting handling derives from the autistic child's behavior, and is not itself the cause of the behavior.

The two groups of families held strikingly different opinions about the services available for their children. Such services were considered inadequate by 39% of the families with an autistic child, as against 17% of families with a nonautistic youngster. This difference in evaluation may be attributed to two circumstances:

1. Physical defects are visible, their nature can be clearly stated, and remedial measures are specific. Autistic be-

havior can be puzzling, and professionals are divided both as to cause and remediation. Hence, parents of autistic children may be referred to inappropriate facilities with disappointing results.

2. Facilities for autistic children are not equipped to deal with youngsters having sensory loss, while those services ready to take the deaf or visually impaired child cannot handle such youngsters if they are also autistic.

Therefore, the family judgment accurately reflects the shortage of facilities for the rubella child who is both autistic and physically defective.

Despite the greater problems facing the families of autistic rubella children, there is no evidence that these children were more rejected. Nor were they viewed less realistically in terms of their physical handicaps. There is thus no significant difference between the two groups in the perception or denial of the physical consequences of congenital rubella.

Maternal attitudes toward these children can, of course, be most complicated. The child's defect is directly due to an illness of the mother, "passed on," so to speak. In many cases an offer of abortion had been refused by the mother. This background clearly creates the possibility that the mother will have irrational feelings of guilt and manifest contradictory rejection and over-protection. The hypothesis of the "schizophrenogenic" mother had to be considered.

The mothers of the autistic children, however, did not differ as a group from the mothers of the nonautistic children. In one instance, on a repeat observation of an autistic youngster 2 years after the initial visit, the younger brother, age 18 months, was present. As the little one behaved in an outgoing, highly related way, the mother remarked, "You have no idea how much pleasure I get from him." She had earlier remarked about her rubella child, "It is very hard to keep trying to make a relationship with a child who doesn't know you exist."

ETIOLOGY

The high prevalence of autism in this series of 243 children with congenital rubella inevitably raises the vexed question of the etiology of childhood autism. Our study did not attempt to probe this question, and we cannot offer a conclusive judgment. Nevertheless, there is an inescapable implication in the data. Our findings would appear to support the argument in favor of an organic etiology as against other lines of inquiry.

On the negative side, we found no evidence to support the psychogenic hypothesis, including the postulate of a schizophrenogenic mother or "refrigerator parents." Nor did genetic components appear implicated, though we made no systematic genetic search. The diversity of families in the sample argues against the possibility that vulnerability to autism is greater in certain socioeconomic groups than in others. The striking individual differences among the retarded children in the group contradicts the speculation that autism is simply a variety of mental subnormality. Any sensory defect in itself cannot explain the autism, in view of the pronounced differences between children with similar handicaps.

The common denominator in our sample is that all the children were at risk for prenatal invasion of the CNS by rubella virus. It seems reasonable to speculate that the common component in our autistic children is brain damage.

This hypothesis is in keeping with the findings of the Baylor University study (Desmond *et al.,* 1967; 1970). In this most detailed investigation of the neurological aftermath of congenital rubella, 8 of the 64 children surviving at 18 months were characterized as autistic. This ratio of autistic to non-autistic rubella children is even higher than in our series. The Baylor study found a wide range of CNS damage in rubella children. The John Hopkins group reported CNS dysfunction in 8 of 33 patients. Rubella virus was recovered from the spinal fluid and brain tissue of several rubella children who died (Hardy *et al.,* 1966).

Our findings are consistent with other current studies that have made neurological assessments of autistic nonrubella children. A survey of 25 autistic children in Western Australia noted that 21 (or 84%) showed some evidence of encephalopathy, and 13 (56%) had unequivocal evidence of organic brain disease (Gubbay *et al.*, 1970). The diagnosis of autism was made according to the "nine point" guide of Creak (1961). All 25 children were retarded.

In Bender's series of 50 autistic children, 28 (or 56%) had organic disorders; and 10 of these 28 had congenital defects (Bender, 1970). Yet even this may not tell the whole story, since Bender notes that the early histories were inadequate for 10 children without apparent organicity and that "the lack of such a history, of course, is not conclusive that some pathology might have existed during pregnancy, birth, or early infancy, either unknown to the parents or not reported by them." Intelligence among the 50 children was low.

In our series, the existence of congenital disorder is unequivocally established. The exact mechanism by which organic damage manifests itself behaviorally as autism remains to be determined. But the association between congenital rubella and autism is striking. One is led to wonder to what extent this link was ignored in the past, especially before the 1964 epidemic made pediatricians and child psychiatrists more aware of the sequelae of rubella.

Certainly it would appear, in view of our findings, that clinicians dealing with autistic behavior in children should routinely inquire whether the mother had rubella during her pregnancy.

10

The Dimension of Temperament

IN INVESTIGATING the behavioral consequences of congenital rubella, we sought not only to diagnose any existing deviances but also to identify characteristics that might foreshadow the development of disturbances at a later age when the children would face more complicated demands.

Studies in both intellectually normal and mentally retarded children have demonstrated that temperament plays a significant role in the etiology of behavior disorders (Thomas *et al.*, 1968; Chess and Korn, 1970). We therefore included in the data collection an assessment of the temperamental attributes of the rubella children to see how this dimension was implicated in their behavioral adaptations.

124

TEMPERAMENTAL ATTRIBUTES

Temperament refers to behavioral style. It describes the characteristic tempo, rhythmicity, energy expenditure, mood, adaptability, and attention focus of a child, independently of the content of any specific behavior. Following are the definitions of the temperamental attributes and the rating scales used in this study, as well as in the New York Longitudinal Study (NYLS), and several other studies.

1. *Activity level* describes the motor component in a child's functioning and the diurnal proportion of active and inactive periods. In scoring this category we use protocol data on motility during eating, playing, dressing, bathing, and handling, as well as information concerning the sleep-wake cycle, reaching, and walking. Rating scale: high, moderate, low.

2. *Rhythmicity* describes the predictability or unpredictability in the timing of functions such as the sleep-wake cycle, hunger, feeding pattern, and elimination. Rating scale: regular, variable, irregular.

3. *Approach-Withdrawal* is the nature of a child's response to a new stimulus, such as an unfamiliar person, food, or toy. Rating scale: approaches, variable, withdraws.

4. *Adaptability* refers to the child's responses to new or altered situations over a period of time. The concern here is not with the nature of the initial responses, but with the speed and ease with which they may be modified in desired directions. Rating scale: adaptive, variable, nonadaptive.

5. *Quality of mood* is the amount of pleasant, joyful, and friendly behavior a child displays as contrasted with unpleasant, unfriendly behavior, and crying. Rating scale: positive, variable, negative.

6. *Intensity of reaction* is the energy level of a child's response, irrespective of its quality or direction. Rating scale: intense, variable, mild.

7. *Threshold of responsiveness* refers to the intensity level of

stimulation required to evoke a discernible response by the child to sensory stimuli, environmental objects, and social contacts. Rating scale: high, moderate, low.

8. *Distractibility* is based on the effectiveness of extraneous environmental stimuli in interfering with or altering the direction of the child's ongoing behavior. Rating scale: distractible, variable, nondistractible.

9. *Attention span and persistence* describe the length of time a particular activity is pursued and the continuation of an activity in the face of obstacles to maintaining the activity direction. Rating scale: persistent, variable, nonpersistent.

Clusters of Traits

The most significant implications of the temperamental characteristics emerge when we consider them not as separate categories but as clusters of traits. Such clusters, or sets of attributes, have been found to be related to the development of behavior disorders and, in school-age youngsters, to academic performance.

One common temperamental constellation comprises regularity, positive approach responses to new stimuli, high adaptability to changes, and pieponderance of positive mood of mild to moderate intensity. A child with these temperamental characteristics develops regular sleep and feeding schedules easily, takes to most new foods at once, smiles at strangers, adapts quickly to a new school, accepts most frustrations with a minimum of fuss, and learns the rules of new games rapidly. Such a youngster is aptly called the "easy child" and is usually a joy to his parents, pediatrician, and teachers. The easy child generally adapts to the demands for socialization with little or no stress and confronts his parents with few, if any, problems in routine handling.

At the opposite end of the temperamental spectrum is the child with irregularity in biological functions, predominantly withdrawal responses to new stimuli, nonadaptability or slow adaptability to change, negative mood, and preponderantly intense reactions. These five temperamental characteristics comprise what we have called the "difficult child" syndrome. The difficult child manifests irregular sleep and feeding patterns, slow acceptance of new foods, prolonged adjustment periods to new routines, and frequent and loud periods of crying. His laughter, too, is characteristically loud. Mothers find such children hard to care for. They are not easy to feed, put to sleep, bathe, or dress. New places, unaccustomed activities, and strange faces may produce initial responses of loud protest or crying. Frustration generally produces a violent tantrum.

We found in the New York Longitudinal Study and in our behavioral study of mentally retarded children that youngsters with the cluster of temperamental traits characteristic of the difficult child accounted for a significantly high proportion of the behavior problem groups, well beyond their representation in each study sample. The specifically stressful demands for these difficult children were shown to be those of socialization, the demands for altering spontaneous responses and patterns to conform to the rules of living of the family, school, or peer group. (Once these children do learn the rules, however, they usually function easily, consistently, and energetically.) As a result of their temperamental characteristics, these children require particularly consistent and objective handling by their parents if maladaptive temperament-environment interactions are to be avoided.

Because of their increased vulnerability to the development of behavior disorders, we felt it would be productive to isolate those rubella youngsters with the characteristics of the difficult child for detailed study and discussion.

Through a structured interview with the mother (or another person responsible for the youngster's daily activity), we obtained a picture of each child's temperament and of the mother's handling techniques in the following areas: wake/sleep, nap, dressing and undressing, eating, soiling and wetting, bathing and washing, sensory and neuromuscular activity, playing, meeting new people and new situations, discipline, illness, verbalization, and crying.

Each descriptive item was scored on a three-point scale, with the first scale point in each category assigned the value 0, the second rating 1, and the third rating 2. A numerical score was then derived to describe the child's temperament in each category.

The Difficult Child

Since we were particularly interested in the cluster of traits describing the difficult child, because of their relationship to the development of behavior disorders, we focused on their distribution among the rubella children. We used the *median* scores of the NYLS children on each of the five crucial temperamental traits (rhythmicity, adaptability, approach/withdrawal, intensity, and mood) as criteria for scoring. Any rubella child whose score for one of these traits fell between this criterion point and the vulnerable extreme was considered to have a "sign" of the difficult child. For example, any child whose score in rhythmicity was between the NYLS median and the polar extreme irregularity was considered to have this temperamental sign of the difficult child.

Using this technique, we then compared the frequency with which the five temperamental characteristics comprising the difficult child syndrome appeared in the rubella children, the Mentally Retarded study children, and the NYLS children at age five (see Table 37).

Although the five signs of the difficult child are found somewhat more often in the rubella children than in the NYLS youngsters and somewhat less often than in the retarded sample, these variations are not statistically significant. Similarly, the distribution of 4, 2, 1 or 0 signs among the three populations is no more than would be expected on the basis of chance alone. Only in the case of three concurrent signs is there a significant difference across the groups, with the NYLS children having a much greater frequency and the retarded and rubella children a slightly lower frequency of their occurrence.

TABLE 37

FREQUENCY OF CONCURRENT SIGNS OF THE "DIFFICULT CHILD" IN THE RUBELLA, NYLS (AT AGE 5), AND MENTALLY RETARDED CHILDREN

No. of Signs	Rubella (N=227)	NYLS (N=105)	Mentally Retarded (N=52)
5	19 (8.4%)	6 (5.7%)	5 (9.6%)
4	43 (19.0%)	19 (18.1%)	10 (19.2%)
3	37 (16.4%)	30 (28.6%)	7 (13.3%)
2	55 (24.3%)	26 (24.8%)	12 (22.9%)
1 or 0	73 (31.9%)	24 (22.9%)	18 (35.0%)

TABLE 38

NUMBER OF SIGNS AND NUMBER OF RUBELLA CHILDREN WITH AND WITHOUT PSYCHIATRIC DISORDER

No. of Signs of the Difficult Child	No Psychiatric Disorder (N=117*) N	%	Psychiatric Disorder (N=110*) N	%
5	6	31.6	13	68.4
4	11	25.6	32	74.4
3	17	44.7	21	55.3
2	27	50.0	27	50.0
1	35	74.5	12	25.5
0	21	80.8	5	19.2

* Only those children for whom temperament could be scored are tabulated here.

In general, therefore, the presence or absence of the signs of the difficult child does not appear to be a meaningful distinction between the groups.

Temperamental Signs and Behavior Disorder

The frequency with which the number of signs of the difficult child are found becomes more important when it is related to the incidence of behavior disorder (Table 38) in the rubella children.

Here we find some particularly striking and significant differences with respect to the children with the maximal or minimal number of signs. Children with two or three signs do not show a distribution among the groups with or without disorder beyond that which would be found by chance. By contrast, almost three-fourths (72.6%) of the youngsters with four or five signs of the difficult child had behavior disorders, and slightly more than three-fourths (76.7%) of the youngsters with zero or one sign had no psychiatric disorder. It thus appears that four or five signs found in combination may be taken as predictive of a certain degree of vulnerability to maladaptive development in these rubella children. Although vulnerability does not constitute inevitability, special handling that recognizes and deals effectively with these "difficult" patterns is likely to be required in order to avoid disorders. On the other hand, while having at most one sign of the difficult child seems to imply the least risk for the development of a behavior disorder, it does not guarantee immunity. Nevertheless, when the so-called "easy children" found in this group show maladaptation, one would have to expect that environmental stress was either very great or of a kind most abrasive to a specific temperamental characteristic. It will be interesting, if follow-up study is done, to see what the psychiatric outcome is in those difficult children now without behavioral symptoms when they are confronted with the greater demands for higher level functioning that accompany school age. In this way we may be able to establish, with increased reliability, the predictive value of these temperamental signs.

Temperament and Physical Defects

As can be seen from Table 39, four or five signs of the difficult child were found in the rubella children with physical defects three times more often than they were in physically intact rubella youngsters (32.0% against 10.2%). The reverse pattern obtains in the case of zero or one signs, although somewhat less dramatically. Here, twice as many children with no defects are temperamentally easy when compared to youngsters with defects. The

TABLE 39

FREQUENCY OF CONCURRENT SIGNS OF THE DIFFICULT CHILD IN RUBELLA CHILDREN WITH OR WITHOUT PHYSICAL DEFECTS (N = 227)

No. of Signs	Rubella Children with No Defects		Rubella Children with Defects	
5	3	(6.1%)	16	(9.0%)
4	2	(4.1%)	41	(23.0%)
3	6	(12.2%)	32	(18.0%)
2	12	(24.5%)	42	(23.6%)
1	14	(28.6%)	33	(18.5%)
0	12	(24.5%)	14	(7.9%)
Total	49	(100%)	178	(100%)

TABLE 40

DEFECTS AND PERCENTAGE OF CHILDREN AT RISK FOR BEHAVIOR PROBLEM DEVELOPMENT

	High Risk (4-5 signs)	Low Risk (0-1 signs)
Children with defects	54.8%	45.2%
Children without defects	16.1%	83.9%

differences between the groups with respect to the incidence of two and three signs are not significant. Thus, in this sample, there does appear to be a relationship between temperament and the presence of physical defect. Damaged youngsters are more frequently found to be difficult, and undamaged children more frequently found to be easy than random distribution of these characteristics would lead one to expect. If children with four and five signs are considered at high risk for the development of behavior disorders and children with zero or one sign are considered at low risk, the implications are highlighted.

As Table 40 indicates, somewhat more than half of the children with defects are at high risk for the development of behavior problems, whereas only about one-sixth of the children without defects are at high risk. These data thus support the findings reached in all our analyses so far—no matter what dimension is being investigated, the handicapped rubella child must be considered particularly vulnerable to maladaptive psychological development, and handling must be geared to avoiding the actualization of this risk.

11

Impact on the Families

IN LOOKING AT THE FAMILIES of these rubella children, we were most interested in the way they understood the child's difficulties, the emotional impact of his presence, the efforts made to communicate with him, their expectations for him, and the changes in previous life style required by his care.

We found that any attempt to characterize the parents' handling of the child as basically permissive, rigid, or flexible made sense in only a few cases. Most of the parents exhibited a variety of behaviors, and to classify them with any conventional labels would be to miss their distinctive character.

Since parents play a crucial role in any child's development during the first years of life, we must clearly understand the nature of the parent-child interaction. Such understanding is especially important when the child is handicapped. So much of what the child will be able to achieve depends upon what he receives from his parents. His defects interfere with his ability to receive stimulation from the environment. The parents therefore have special responsibilities for mediating between the child and his surroundings. At the same time, the amount the parents are able to give will depend to a large extent on what they receive from the child. A handicapped child may be unable to provide what a parent might expect by way of emotional expressiveness or developmental progress, and yet the parent is expected to give so much more than a normal child might require. In such a situation, how extraordinarily difficult a mutually rewarding interaction may be.

FAMILIES' UNDERSTANDING OF CHILDREN'S DIFFICULTIES

During their interview with the social worker, parents were asked to identify their child's defects. Almost all had a clear understanding of the youngster's sensory defects and physical handicaps but a very confused picture of the behavioral consequences, even the most obvious ones, of these disorders. For instance, parents who understood that their child could not hear worried about his lack of speech and tended to see this as either a separate defect or as due to mental retardation. Similarly, parents who knew that their child was brain damaged were not aware that hyperactivity, aimless behavior, attentional difficulties, or impulse disorders were behavioral consequences to be expected. The problem seemed to be not that the parents were given an unclear explanation of the diagnosis and its effects but that they were unable to absorb the information. Even when parents were told in detail what to expect, they often did not objectively assimilate the facts as they pertained to their child, but rather incorporated the information in a way that fulfilled their own needs and expectations.

This lack of assimilation may partly be due to the variety of sources from which the parents got information at different stages of the child's development. They interpreted the various reports according to their own needs. Some parents completely disregarded the presence of obvious speech defects as a consequence of rubella because they remembered that in the original examination all they were told was that the child had some visual difficulties. They spoke at length about the speech problem as a "family pattern" that would magically disappear at a later age, with no need for remedial services.

In addition, some parents chose to ignore certain defects because the multiplicity was overwhelming—they just could not list how many things had gone wrong with the child. Many merely said the child had a visual or hearing defect, gave a quantitative appraisal of the defect, and were unable to give a qualitative picture of what this meant in terms of daily living. Some parents knew their child well and described what he could and could not do in terms of seeing or hearing. Others kept repeating a general statement that the child was profoundly deaf and that was all.

Profound deafness with the consequent lack of speech was the defect that bothered the parents most. This is not surprising, since deafness was the most common handicap. Many parents felt that without speech the child just wouldn't be able to make it through life and that his dependency on them would be unending. Furthermore, the impact of this defect on the parents became greater as the child grew up. A four-year-old without speech was excluded from play with other youngsters, whereas a younger child could do well with friends, since speech was not crucial to their activities.

In many cases, the rubella infant was the couple's first child (39% of the children were first born). Added to the normal anxieties of young parents facing baby care for the first time was the often devastating fact that the infant required extra skills that they had neither the time nor ability to develop. Many parents concentrated on the aspect of the child's defect that hit them the hardest and spent themselves emotionally in trying to deal with it. Thus, some said it was distressing that the child would never experience sorrow, happiness, and other human feelings. As one mother put it, "If you can't have that, what else is there that gives sense to life?" For others, the fact that the child would never hear life's many sounds was most disturbing.

The mothers were troubled about the care they had taken during pregnancy. They wondered, "If I had been more cautious, would I have been able to detect rubella in time for the doctor to terminate the pregnancy?" Thus, compounding the tragedy of having a handicapped child were feelings of guilt, varying in degree from parent to parent. In many instances, parents were able to relax after the birth of another child gave them reassurance that they could produce a normal human being. Other parents were so terrified by what they knew rationally could almost never happen again, and had such intense guilt and fear, that they decided not to have other children.

The sense of guilt was often a major factor in the relationship between husband and wife—had they done enough to prevent this misfortune? In one family the issue was: should the mother, a schoolteacher, have stopped teaching as soon as she became pregnant, avoiding potential contact with rubella? Guilt also influenced the parents' relationship with other children in the family. Many mothers were torn about how much time should be taken up by the rubella child and how much time given to normal sibs. Some parents felt that if the child couldn't learn, why should they insist on his making the effort? But others, just because it was so hard for the child to learn, felt obliged to spend all their time working with him to master what was necessary.

Emotional problems also developed between husband and wife. A mother often had ways of handling and communicating with a child that the father, having less time to spend with him, did not grasp. Quite often, the husband had so little access to the world created by child and mother that he came to think his rubella son would not develop the proper identification as a male and blamed this on the mother. Such a father frequently expected his four-year-old son to display a strong sexual identification, in terms of roles and choice of play, that he would not necessarily have pushed so hard for in a normal child.

As a child grew older, difficulties piled up for the parents. In many instances, they were not given a definitive diagnosis of the child's defects in the neonatal period. Rather, each time they brought the child for an appointment they were told about something else that was wrong with him. This was the result of the ongoing nature of the rubella infection as well as the fact that some abnormalities, such as hearing loss, could not be accurately evaluated in a very young child.

The fact that these children showed little or no progress in overcoming a handicap as they grew older was hard for the parents to accept. Despite their efforts, a child might not exhibit any advance in his activities. Since this lack of progress was apparent to others, it became a source of embarrassment as well as concern.

In some families, the negative emotional impact of having a handicapped child was partly offset by the fact that the parents could refer to a specific disease and a highly publicized epidemic, and therefore did not have to torture themselves figuring out what had happened to cause their child's defects. Also, the disruptive influence of having a damaged child in the home was in some cases counterbalanced by the fact that the parent was left busy finding and securing services for the child, thereby using his energies productively.

FAMILIES' HANDLING OF CHILDREN

The defect found most frequently was hearing loss, either by itself or in combination with other defects; and lack of speech in the children was one of the main problems for the parents. Many felt that without speech the child lacked what was basic for his being able to function adequately. They assumed that the child's difficulty with words meant that he had difficulty thinking. Often, as a result, they felt that certain situations were too complicated for the child, did not explain them to him, and thus deprived the child of the possibility of new experiences.

The use of gestures was an important issue for many of the parents, especially those whose children attended schools or clinics which advised discouraging gestures in order to strengthen the possibility of the child's using language. These parents had been told that any child who is understood when he uses gestures will not feel the need for using the corresponding words.

However, as we have already noted in Chapter 6, gesturing can be an important means of communication between parent and child, and it was our impression that those children who did use gestures developed a more meaningful level of communication. What was of utmost importance was the fact of communication, and the means used were only secondary.

The parents reported various kinds of ideas that were most difficult to communicate to the deaf child. Some said that it was hardest to communicate any abstract idea. Others found that the most difficult thing was to explain in advance a new experience, for example, a trip to the zoo for the first time. They were constantly frustrated in their efforts to build up the child's expectations. Other parents felt it was important to give the children religious feelings, but didn't know how. Many commented on feelings of helplessness in communicating their values and attitudes.

Another difficulty arose when the parents tried to communicate the need to be cautious in certain situations. Even though a child had been hurt the first time he went out on the fire escape, the fear of being hurt again didn't stop him from going out again, and the parents felt powerless to deal with the problem. Those hyperactive children who climbed over everything in the home would continue to do so no matter how many times they fell.

While it is true that children in general show individual differences in their readiness to learn appropriate caution, these youngsters as a group appear to learn more slowly. This may be understood in terms of brain dysfunction or retardation, but it still may leave parents feeling helpless and frustrated.

Some parents, knowing their child was deaf, decided on their own to reduce his activities to an elementary level and to teach him simple ways to convey his needs. Automatically assuming that when the child was fussy he either wanted to eat or go to the bathroom, they taught the child two basic gestures as signals for eating and toileting. Whenever he fussed, they expected him to communicate his needs with these gestures. They did not really expect higher functioning from him. Some went even further. They would leave cookies on a table so the child could take them himself and not even have to express his need for them. For the most part, such parents equated talking with thinking. They believed that since the child couldn't do one he couldn't do the other.

In general, the parents were told by various specialists to talk to the children. Most understood that this continuous stimulation was vital, even if the child could not talk back to them. However, this was at times a most difficult task. Just getting the child's attention so that they could attempt to communicate through speech was a chore which did not always meet with success. It was difficult to tell whether the failure was due to the child's absorption in what he was doing, his deliberate pretending not to hear, or his actual inability to hear.

Among the discipline problems mentioned by the parents were the children's stubbornness and determination to have their own way. It was so difficult to divert them from what they wanted to do that physical restriction was often necessary. This troubled the parents, because while they could physically restrain a three- or four-year-old, they did not know what to do with an older child. They felt that if they could explain the reasons for a certain rule it would make discipline easier, but since the child had no speech, this was impossible.

Many of the parents centered their complaints on their child's hyperactivity, since destructiveness was a frequent consequence of his behavior. It was not unusual for a child, while in seemingly perpetual motion, to break objects, empty drawers, turn over furniture, throw things on the floor. For the most part, this destructiveness was an unmotivated consequence of the child's activity level.

Parents were also faced with the problem of how much to expect from the child. Some became rigid, setting up rules that had to be obeyed without exception. If the youngster, handicapped or not, didn't obey, he would be punished. Others went to the other extreme and adopted a laissez-faire attitude: why restrain the child since he already has so many burdens to carry? These parents might then permit the child to control the household by his behavior. Disagreements between the mother and father or inconsistencies in the same parent were quite common when it came to determining ways of handling the child.

We found that the families' attitudes toward training the children were related to the number of defect areas involved. With an increase in the number of defects the child had, the families were less likely to be flexible and more likely to be "permissive." We judged permissiveness not in absolute terms, but in relation to the child's actual functional capacity and his ability to learn restrictions and positive patterns of behavior. Parents were sometimes amazed by how much discipline their child could accept when he began to attend nursery school. They were also surprised that such discipline, intelligently applied, could actually improve the child's responsiveness to learning situations.

As already noted in the chapter on levels of functioning, there was a marked discrepancy between what the children in our sample were capable of doing and what they routinely did. This discrepancy imposed heavy demands on the parents for assistance. Some parents enjoyed giving this kind of assistance and spoke of their four-year-old as "my baby." They encouraged the child to have a prolonged babyhood because they liked to feel needed. Such handling kept the child from developing the skills necessary for independence. Other parents were depressed and resentful about their role as caretakers of a child who showed almost no progress.

Parents found the most problems in the area of toileting, especially with their three- and four-year-olds. The emphasis given to toilet-training by society makes it harder to accept lack of self-care in this area than in other daily routines such as feeding or dressing. Many rubella children seemed unable to learn how to signal their need to eliminate, and this underlay their inability to become trained. Parents felt angry and depressed at lack of success in this area.

Two-thirds of the children displayed unusual habits or rituals that the parents found most frustrating to handle. Among the most common of these were the mouthing and chewing of objects, spinning in circles, plucking eyelids, gazing at lights, smelling all objects, and head banging. These activities represented "crazy behavior" to the parents, and they often didn't mention them spontaneously to an interviewer because they couldn't imagine that they might be part of the rubella syndrome. Instead, they blamed themselves, believing that the strange actions resulted from their handling of the child.

The high incidence of stereotyped and ritualistic behavior in these children may reflect mannerisms typical of children with visual and hearing defects, or they may possibly be consequences of retardation and brain dysfunction. To parents, however, these were behaviors that made their children socially unacceptable. A causal relationship between rubella and deafness could be explained to oneself or others, but where was the connection between having had rubella and chewing matches or smelling feet? The parents tried to figure out how they could stop such behavior. Their attempts to engage the child in a substitute activity often had discouraging results.

The parents' concern about the child's future was somewhat

limited, probably owing to their deep involvement in problems of the here and now. Several asked if their child would be able to learn to read. Only infrequently, however, did parents express worry over the youngster's later job-holding capability and possibility of marrying. (It is of interest to note that these were prominent worries of the parents of mentally retarded children we investigated in a separate study.)

The overwhelming desire was for the rubella children to be able in general to live, learn, and work in the normal world. At the time of the study, many of the children were attending special nursery schools or programs. While the parents appreciated these as necessary for appropriate training, they all hoped that eventually the youngsters could somehow make their way in the world of the non-handicapped, even if on a limited basis.

The responses to the presence of a defective rubella child in the family varied widely, from demoralization with regard to the parental role to a close and more compassionate relationship stemming from the cooperative effort required to meet the child's needs.

Several bewildered young couples have definitely decided against having any more children. In one such family, the husband and wife had been childhood sweethearts in Puerto Rico and had come to New York as a newly married couple. During the first weeks of pregnancy, the young woman had rubella. But the couple were unaware of what this might mean. They met no Spanish-speaking personnel in the prenatal clinic. The danger to the child became known only during the second trimester of pregnancy, too late for an abortion, the doctors judged. But little of this was understood by the patient or her husband. At the time of our parental interview, done in Spanish, the father of the badly damaged child still would not believe any statement that this catastrophe could not recur, and that another baby would have every chance of being normal. The young mother spent her days holding in her arms a four-year, three-month-old boy whose total adaptation was under a one-year level, showing not only profound mental retardation but also severe deafness and bilateral cataracts.

This experience was duplicated in one or another degree by other families, especially when the rubella child was the first born. In place of the anticipated pleasure in their offspring, energies were taken up by numerous diagnostic appointments, taking the defective child to special nurseries, admitting him to a hospital for cardiac or eye surgery, attending hearing and speech centers. In some cases, because parents and/or siblings were embarrassed to be seen in public with the rubella child, the family experienced social isolation.

The change in life style was less drastic in several families. Many of these were large families with good interrelatedness antedating the birth of the rubella child. Older siblings were on hand to carry on household duties and look after younger brothers and sisters during the mother's many absences. The healthy patterns of development of these other children mitigated the disappointments and worries over the defective child.

The negative social consequences of fetal rubella to the families, though impressive now, may seem mild in comparison with those to come. Most of our study children were of preschool age. When they reach the age of compulsory school attendance, a new set of stresses will arise for both them and the parents. From studies of mentally retarded children we have learned that the social rejection of a defective child becomes most prominent at the age when the neighborhood children play together outdoors after school hours and on weekends. These periods highlight the youngster's inability to participate on an equal level in various games, and he commonly reacts to rejection with withdrawal, aggression, and a host of other defensive maneuvers.

In addition, as these rubella children get older, the problem of locating a proper educational facility will sharpen. For those youngsters attending a special day school for the deaf or registered in a residential school for the blind with weekends at home, negative social impact will be temporarily limited to functioning outside of school. For those enrolled in regular school, even if in special classes, the deviations in cognitive skills with or without sensory defect will make for problems in educational placement. The goal should be an educational placement that provides the best learning situation without surrounding the youngster with such a special environment that he fails to develop skills for dealing with the normal world to the extent of his capacities.

It appeared that the parents did not expect the clinic or remedial services to be concerned with their family problems, which in many instances arose from the presence of the damaged child. Nor did they view the hospital clinic as a place to air complaints about behavior, or to seek guidance for coping with such problems as came to notice during the course of this study.

Our analysis of the services given to rubella families points up the great need for correlating various aspects of the child's health care. We noted a tendency to segment the general area of physical defects and the social and educational consequences of these defects. In addition, some of the parents were bewildered by the seemingly contradictory advice concerning management of the child that they received from medical consultants, special clinics, and schools. This points to the need both for coordinating the care that the child receives and for centralizing information given to the parents.

12

Overview

THIS IS THE FIRST detailed study of the behavioral consequences of congenital rubella in so large a group of children. We hope that studies in other centers will provide additional data to enlarge our understanding of this important issue. As we review our own findings on this group of 243 youngsters, we note the recurrence of several major concepts that merit special emphasis. These concepts and their implications for effective management of rubella children may be summed up as follows.

1) Congenital rubella is a disease that involves many body organs and results in a wide range of defects. The multiple physical findings are accompanied by a diversity of behavioral manifestations. The concept of "the multihandicapped child" has

145

to be grasped in order to comprehend the problem of most rubella children. Their difficulties cannot be understood if one accepts the prevailing tendency to pigeonhole a child in terms of one defect. It is a gross oversimplification to view the rubella child as "simply" deaf or "simply" retarded. Different combinations of defect may have their own specific consequences for the child's functioning. Each additional pathology does not merely add a new component, but also changes all other factors. The addition of mental retardation, for example, to the problem of deafness makes for entirely different problems of adaptation than the combination of blindness and deafness, or mental retardation plus autism in a deaf child. The pathologies interact and potentiate each other, and the whole is greater than the sum of its parts.

This study reveals a definite correlation between the number of physical defects and the presence of psychiatric disorder in the rubella child. The more physical handicaps he has, the more likely he is to display coexistent behavioral pathology. Thus, among the 50 children in our sample who had no apparent physical defects, the incidence of behavioral deviation was comparable to that in any random group of their age. At the opposite pole, only one of the 27 children with defects in four physical areas was free of psychiatric problems. While recognizing this correlation, we must guard against the assumption that there is a necessary and inevitable relationship between physical and behavioral sequelae, since 47 children with two or more areas of physical defect were free of psychiatric pathology.

For proper management, the multihandicapped rubella child requires facilities that go beyond the single or double purposes (deaf or deaf-blind) for which they are now designed. Facilities must be restructured to deal with multiple issues that may arise with certain children.

2) Congenital rubella is not only a multisystem disease, but also a continuing disease. Because of the ongoing nature of the infection, the rubella syndrome is not a static one. One must

reckon with the possibility of new manifestations as time goes by. It is therefore imperative to have continued evaluations so that defects not immediately evident at birth (such as central nervous system damage or hearing loss) are not overlooked and the etiology of difficulties developing later is clarified.

In the same way, changes in behavioral manifestations over time must be watched for. This makes it all the more necessary to have a flexible approach to handling of the child. It may become necessary to reassign him to a new facility as changes appear in the dominant character of his disability. Unfortunately, there is no adequate model at present for dealing with the multi-handicapped child who may develop additional unanticipated handicaps resulting from the same central focus of disease.

3) That mental retardation is one of the major consequences of congenital rubella is underscored by the fact that over one-third of our children (37%) had varying degrees of retardation. Since the expected prevalence in the general population is 2 to 3%, the startling difference can reasonably be ascribed to the prenatal infection. It is also noteworthy that most cases of mental retardation in the general population fall into the borderline and mild categories, whereas most rubella children are in the severe and profound categories. Thus it is obvious that if a rubella epidemic should ever strike again, we would need to be prepared with facilities appropriate to the needs of many significantly retarded children. These would not necessarily be psychiatric facilities, since only 71% of the mentally retarded rubella children manifested behavioral pathology other than could be accounted for by their lowered cognitive capacities and developmental levels. We must recognize, however, that as these children grow out of the preschool period they will be at risk for the development of behavior disorders. They will be subjected to greater stress. Moreover, continuation of certain behaviors, such as speech difficulties and occasional tantrums, not now classified as disorders, may require a psychiatric reassessment.

4) Distortions of thought processes and delays in cognitive advances have mainly occurred in children with physical signs of virological invasion of various body systems. This close association lends weight to the possibility that the end-organ defect reflects central nervous system damage.

Because deafness is such a prominent finding in rubella children (nearly three-fourths of our sample had hearing loss), the behavioral consequences of deafness merit careful study, particularly in anticipation of future problems. Behaviors described as characteristic of some deaf adults include rigidity, lack of impulse control, perseveration, and difficulty in changing set of mind (Rainer *et al.*, 1969). Since these characteristics are highly correlated with those found in brain-damaged individuals, it has been suggested that a higher proportion of deaf people than is generally recognized may have brain damage in addition to their end-organ defect. This question has been raised with regard to our deaf rubella children by the Hearing and Speech clinic as a result of their experiences in repeated evaluations. While some of the youngsters have a clearly definable degree of deafness and respond in an organized social manner to sounds when they are given hearing aids, there is another group in whom the degree of hearing loss is most difficult to assess. These youngsters have varying responses within the same testing session or from one test to another. A therapeutic trial with a prosthesis is equally puzzling, resulting in such inconsistent responses that it has been postulated that CNS damage may be interfering with the symbolic meaning of the sounds.

The question is not simply one of determining whether the deafness is mild, moderate, severe, or profound; nor is it simply a matter of supplying the proper hearing aid. Those deaf children who are brain damaged will also have a number of difficulties adversely affecting their ability to learn in formal school work and to develop social skills. This handicap will mark them as odd, unable to deal with the ordinary give and take of interpersonal peer relations. Not only is there a need for early identification of central brain involvement, but also for mapping the details of a child's malfunction so that special educational arrangements can be made before failures have piled up and maladaptive defensive behaviors have developed, further complicating the problem.

We have hints that these factors are beginning to assert themselves with regard to some rubella children.

5) The proportion of autistic children in this group was strikingly high, far in excess of the incidence reported in the general population. Ten children were diagnosed as autistic in the full classical sense, and eight others as manifesting a partial syndrome of autism. Since the label of autism has often been used too loosely, we would emphasize that our criteria for this diagnosis were rigorous. In addition to the 18 youngsters identified as autistic, there were a number whose behavior patterns strongly suggested autistic tendencies. But wherever rituals and mannerisms in sensorially damaged children were typical of their sensory defect (for example, deaf mannerisms and blindisms), we have assumed in the absence of other behavioral deviations that the sensory defect was the cause of the pathological behavior.

It is possible, however, that in some of these children the basic explanation for their deviant behavior was autism, with the specific form of mannerisms determined by the fact of sensory loss. This question may later be clarified by examining such a child's total adaptation at age levels when wider repertoires of normative behaviors are to be expected. We will then be in a better position to assess deviances in affective relatedness as well as the degree of fixity of the ritualistic patterns and their use as a barrier to human interaction.

Our findings of an association between congenital rubella and autism would appear to support the view that autism has an organic etiology. The findings suggest that clinicians dealing with autistic behavior should look into the possibility that the mother had rubella during pregnancy. Conversely, one must be alert to the possibility that a child known to have congenital rubella may develop autistic behavior. It would clearly be a mistake to treat such behavior as a purely psychological manifestation.

6) As in previous studies with both normative and mentally retarded groups of children, we have found it useful to consider the temperamental qualities, or individual behavioral styles, of rubella children. The data on temperament reported here indicate that the characteristic activity level, rhythmicity, mood, intensity, and attention focus of a child may be implicated in his behavioral adaptations. The clusters of traits that identify "the difficult child," in particular, are in certain cases predictive of vulnerability to maladaptive development and should signal the need for special handling. However, the full significance of the data on temperament in this group of children will be known only when follow-up studies are done.

7) With rubella children, as with other handicapped children, one must not mistake optimum capacity for routine ability. We have therefore sought to determine the child's daily level of performance, as concretely observed, rather than relying on reports of his maximum performance. This distinction has practical importance. Only by understanding apparent discrepancies in the child's levels of functioning can parents and teachers realistically judge what demands and expectations are appropriate. On the one hand, demands for daily functioning based on a child's sporadic bursts of top activity may produce excessive stress and lead to psychiatric difficulty, compounding the child's handicap. On the other hand, mere acquiescence in a level of performance far below the child's capacity may stunt his developmental possibilities. An attempt must be made to bring up the level of routine functioning as close as possible to the child's potential. For the multihandicapped child, the effort to maintain this evaluative balance is no less important than for other children.

8) Social factors play an important part in congenital rubella and its sequelae. The partiality of the infective agent is as much an issue as in tuberculosis, which has always struck especially hard at the poor. This is clearly suggested by the overrepresentation in our study population of children from Puerto Rican families. Living in crowded slum conditions increased the chances that a pregnant woman would be in contact with rubella. A communication barrier, in the absence of a special educational campaign in Spanish, prevented some pregnant women from becoming alerted to the danger until it was too late for an abortion. And for other women, at a time when abortion was still illegal for reasons other than a threat to the mother's life, obtaining an abortion required more sophistication and money than their low-income family could command. The obvious lesson of this experience is the need for action specifically aimed at making knowledge and facilities available to underprivileged socioeconomic groups.

9) On the families of rubella children, the disease has a powerful impact, psychologically and socially. A special comment should be made about the fact that 39% of our study children were first born. When parents have already had a normal child, the grief attendant upon the birth of a defective child is still very real. But the devastation of the parents whose first baby is born with multiple handicaps is all the more dramatic. Insecurities about personal competence often come to the fore at the time of a first pregnancy, with fantasies that the child may be born defective. When such fears were confirmed, some parents in our group determined not to have any more children. Their anxieties were so pervasive that they could not be reassured; they were firmly convinced that their next child would also be born retarded, deaf, and blind.

The anxieties of the families were very much associated with the degree to which a child's special needs were being met by available facilities. And this in turn depended to a large extent

on whether the youngster's cluster of handicaps—or single defect
—represented a need already recognized by the community and
therefore planned for by special programs. Certain handicaps,
particularly those involving hard-to-handle behavior patterns, are
often not recognized as a legitimate educational responsibility but
rather appear to school personnel as nuisances interfering with the
performance of their proper functions. For example, it is recognized that deaf children should be taught. A school which has
a deaf child knows that he should either be included in a
special class or be given special handling in a normal class. But
if a deaf child is a behavior problem as well, the parents are
likely to be told that this is something *they* must do something
about so as to eliminate its intrusion into the classroom. The
problem is not viewed as a challenge to the educators to be dealt
with collaboratively by school and parents. There is the same
question with each specific cluster of rubella handicaps—if appropriate facilities are not available, a sense of helplessness on
the part of those who run the facilities leads them to tell the
parents, "Your child does not belong here." Where he does belong
is left to the parents to find out.

One of the clearest messages of our study is that parents
with a multihandicapped youngster can find themselves so over-
burdened with clinic or doctor visits, each addressed to a different aspect of the problem, that they must often make a choice
between their defective child's needs and those of their normal
healthy children. Then, when the many pilgrimages are duly
carried out, the families often receive advice which seems to be
—and often in fact is—contradictory. Each specialist, addressing
himself to one aspect of the youngster's problems may prescribe
a regimen that contraverts another need of the child. The piling
up of recommended procedures may reach such unwieldy propor-
tions that the parent may have to make an arbitrary choice on his
own.

In view of the special nature and complexity of the rubella
child's problems, parent guidance from a central source is impera-

tive. Parents find it hard to understand the "crazy behavior" of some rubella children. They are often bewildered and at a loss to deal with such ritualistic behavior as endless twirling or the meaningless smelling of feet. The family needs to be told what such conduct means, how it is related to the rubella infection, and how it can be handled. If the parent is not helped to anticipate such behavior, his bafflement and sense of shame are understandable. The presence of a rubella child has an effect on the entire family and their way of life. They are entitled to professional counsel on coping with the problem.

10) Finally, the need for follow-up studies of these rubella children is urgent. A thread that runs through our report is uncertainty about their future. We are not at all sure that the behavioral damage caused by the rubella virus has been completely assessed. For we have studied the children only in their preschool period. In this period the social aspects of physical and behavioral handicaps are marginal. The youngsters are still within the protecting atmosphere of the family circle. When they are included in a nursery or play group, any known physical or behavioral deviations can be taken into account in their handling. Noxious attitudes of other children or even adults can be contained and their effects modified. But as the youngsters grow older it becomes less possible and advisable to maintain such an atmosphere. In general, one wishes the child to function in the most normal situations in which he can develop constructive coping devices and healthy interactions. This is not always easy to achieve. One can either overestimate or underestimate both the degree of stress and the child's capacity to master stresses in a healthy manner. Some of the answers to this question of the social aspects of both physical and behavioral handicaps will only be found in a follow-up investigation of the youngsters.

A second major reason for follow-up studies has to do with the adequacy of our instruments for identifying cerebral maldevelopment. We have tried to be parsimonious and rigorous in our diagnosis of "cerebral dysfunction." The normative rate of development of various behavioral capacities has a wide range, and it is therefore hard to be certain that suspected deviations are in fact indicative of brain maldevelopment. However, as the children reach ages in which more is expected of their cognitive capacities, affective relatedness, impulse control, and integrated functioning, it will become more possible to identify a fault in one or more capacities. Defective development of visual-motor or auditory-motor abilities may first clearly appear in the context of formal learning tasks. In the early grades it becomes possible to identify inabilities to coordinate intersensory stimuli (for example auditory-visual, visual-tactile), to select significant details from a background matrix of facts, to integrate details into a whole. These and other cognitive capacities must wait for assessment until the youngsters have reached an age when their responses to school demands will show either integrity or defect.

In a similar way, formal social situations or activities outside of the home may highlight problems of impulse control or affective deviations that were obscured in a household which either had habituated itself to the handicapped child or had fed him only stimuli and demands to which he could respond appropriately. There are times when family history reveals the fact of behavioral immaturity or aberration in the very protestations of normality, because the illustrations of normality are so clearly examples of ineffectual functioning or reduced expectations.

We have tried to anticipate external stresses and children's responses to stresses at older ages, as well as the emerging indices of cerebral dysfunction, by including data that may be predictive of disorders of brain integration. Whether or not we have done so sufficiently will have to await follow-up studies on these children.

Appendix A

Correlation of Psychiatric Diagnoses with Kind,
Number, and Severity of Physical Defects

SINGLE DEFECT: HEARING

Hearing, Unspecified

No Psychiatric Disorder	1
Reactive Behavior Disorder	2
Cerebral Dysfunction + Mental Retardation + Partial Syndrome of Autism	1
Total	4

Hearing, Moderate

No Psychiatric Disorder	7
Reactive Behavior Disorder	3
Mental Retardation, Severe	1
Reactive Behavior Disorder + Cerebral Dysfunction + Mental Retardation	1
Reactive Behavior Disorder + Mental Retardation, Borderline	1
Mental Retardation, Unspecified + Partial Syndrome of Autism	1
Total	14

Hearing, Severe

No Psychiatric Disorder	31
Reactive Behavior Disorder	7
Cerebral Dysfunction	1
Mental Retardation, Borderline	3
Mental Retardation, Moderate	2
Partial Syndrome of Autism	1
Mental Retardation, Unspecified + Autism	1
Mental Retardation, Moderate + Autism	1
Total	47

SINGLE DEFECT: VISUAL

Visual, Moderate

Reactive Behavior Disorder	1
Mental Retardation, Severe	1
Total	2

Visual, Severe

No Psychiatric Disorder	1
Mental Retardation, Severe	1
Total	2

SINGLE DEFECT: NEUROLOGICAL

Mental Retardation, Mild	1
Total	1

SINGLE DEFECT: CARDIAC

No Psychiatric Disorder	1
Reactive Behavior Disorder	1
Total	2

DOUBLE DEFECT: HEARING PLUS VISUAL

Hearing Unspecified, Visual Moderate

Mental Retardation, Borderline	1
Total	1

Hearing Unspecified, Visual Severe
Mental Retardation, Profound   1
Mental Retardation, Moderate + Partial Syndrome of Autism   1
                                                                     ──
                                                     Total   2

Hearing Moderate, Visual Mild
No Psychiatric Disorder   1
                                                                     ──
                                                     Total   1

Hearing Moderate, Visual Moderate
No Psychiatric Disorder   1
Mental Retardation, Mild   1
Mental Retardation, Unspecified + Partial Syndrome of Autism   1
                                                                     ──
                                                     Total   3

Hearing Severe, Visual Mild
No Psychiatric Disorder   1
Mental Retardation, Borderline   1
                                                                     ──
                                                     Total   2

Hearing Severe, Visual Moderate
No Psychiatric Disorder   3
Mental Retardation, Severe   1
                                                                     ──
                                                     Total   4

Hearing Severe, Visual Severe
Mental Retardation, Moderate   1
                                                                     ──
                                                     Total   1

DOUBLE DEFECT: HEARING PLUS NEUROLOGICAL

Hearing Unspecified, Neurological
No Psychiatric Disorder   1
                                                                     ──
                                                     Total   1

Hearing Moderate, Neurological

No Psychiatric Disorder 3
Mental Retardation, Mild 1

                                                        Total   4

Hearing Severe, Neurological

No Psychiatric Disorder 4
Reactive Behavior Disorder 2
Cerebral Dysfunction 1
Mental Retardation, Moderate 2
Mental Retardation, Severe 3
Mental Retardation, Moderate + Partial Syndrome of Autism   1

                                                        Total   13

DOUBLE DEFECT: HEARING PLUS CARDIAC

Hearing Unspecified, Cardiac

Reactive Behavior Disorder 1

                                                        Total   1

Hearing Moderate, Cardiac

No Psychiatric Disorder 5

                                                        Total   5

Hearing Severe, Cardiac

No Psychiatric Disorder 3
Mental Retardation, Severe + Autism 1

                                                        Total   4

DOUBLE DEFECT: VISUAL PLUS NEUROLOGICAL

Visual Mild, Neurological

Mental Retardation, Severe 1

                                                        Total   1

DOUBLE DEFECT: VISUAL PLUS CARDIAC

Visual Moderate, Cardiac
Reactive Behavior Disorder   1
                                                              —
                                                    Total   1

Visual Severe, Cardiac
No Psychiatric Disorder   1
                                                              —
                                                    Total   1

DOUBLE DEFECT: NEUROLOGICAL PLUS CARDIAC

Neurological, Cardiac
No Psychiatric Disorder   1
Mental Retardation, Severe   1
                                                              —
                                                    Total   2

TRIPLE DEFECT: HEARING PLUS VISUAL PLUS
NEUROLOGICAL

Hearing Unspecified, Visual Mild, Neurological
Mental Retardation, Moderate   1
                                                              —
                                                    Total   1

Hearing Moderate, Visual Severe, Neurological
Mental Retardation, Severe   1
                                                              —
                                                    Total   1

Hearing Severe, Visual Mild, Neurological
No Psychiatric Disorder   1
                                                              —
                                                    Total   1

Hearing Severe, Visual Moderate, Neurological
No Psychiatric Disorder   1
Cerebral Dysfunction + Mental Retardation   1
Mental Retardation, Unspecified   1
Mental Retardation, Moderate   1
Mental Retardation, Unspecified + Partial Syndrome of Autism   1
                                                              —
                                                    Total   5

Hearing Severe, Visual Severe, Neurological

Cerebral Dysfunction + Mental Retardation	1
Mental Retardation, Severe	1
Mental Retardation, Profound	1
Total	3

TRIPLE DEFECT: HEARING PLUS VISUAL PLUS CARDIAC

Hearing Unspecified, Visual Moderate, Cardiac

Reactive Behavior Disorder	1
Mental Retardation, Moderate	1
Total	2

Hearing Moderate, Visual Moderate, Cardiac

Mental Retardation, Mild	1
Mental Retardation, Moderate	1
Total	2

Hearing Severe, Visual Moderate, Cardiac

No Psychiatric Disorder	2
Reactive Behavior Disorder	2
Mental Retardation, Mild	1
Mental Retardation, Severe	1
Mental Retardation, Unspecified + Autism	1
Mental Retardation, Borderline + Autism	1
Autism	1
Total	9

Hearing Severe, Visual Severe, Cardiac

Mental Retardation, Borderline	1
Mental Retardation, Severe	1
Mental Retardation, Profound	2
Total	4

TRIPLE DEFECT: HEARING PLUS NEUROLOGICAL PLUS CARDIAC

Hearing Unspecified, Neurological, Cardiac

No Psychiatric Disorder	1
Mental Retardation, Severe	1
Total	2

Hearing Moderate, Neurological, Cardiac
No Psychiatric Disorder   2
                                                                                              —
                                                                      Total   2

Hearing Severe, Neurological, Cardiac
No Psychiatric Disorder   5
Cerebral Dysfunction + Mental Retardation   1
Mental Retardation, Mild   1
Mental Retardation, Moderate   1
Mental Retardation, Severe   1
Reactive Behavior Disorder + Cerebral Dysfunction + Mental
    Retardation   1
Mental Retardation, Severe + Autism   1
                                                                                              —
                                                                      Total   11

TRIPLE DEFECT: VISUAL PLUS NEUROLOGICAL PLUS CARDIAC

Visual Moderate, Neurological, Cardiac
Reactive Behavior Disorder + Mental Retardation, Borderline   1
                                                                                              —
                                                                      Total   1

Visual Severe, Neurological, Cardiac
Mental Retardation, Severe   1
Mental Retardation, Profound   2
                                                                                              —
                                                                      Total   3

QUADRUPLE DEFECTS

Hearing Unspecified, Visual Mild, Neurological, Cardiac
Mental Retardation, Borderline + Autism   1
                                                                                              —
                                                                      Total   1

Hearing Unspecified, Visual Moderate, Neurological, Cardiac
Mental Retardation, Severe   1
                                                                                              —
                                                                      Total   1

Hearing Unspecified, Visual Severe, Neurological, Cardiac

Mental Retardation, Severe	2
Mental Retardation, Profound	3
Total	5

Hearing Moderate, Visual Moderate, Neurological, Cardiac

Mental Retardation, Severe	3
Reactive Behavior Disorder + Mental Retardation, Severe	1
Total	4

Hearing Moderate, Visual Severe, Neurological, Cardiac

Mental Retardation, Moderate	1
Mental Retardation, Severe	1
Total	2

Hearing Severe, Visual Mild, Neurological, Cardiac

Mental Retardation, Moderate	1
Total	1

Hearing Severe, Visual Moderate, Neurological, Cardiac

No Psychiatric Disorder	1
Reactive Behavior Disorder	1
Mental Retardation, Mild	1
Mental Retardation, Moderate	1
Mental Retardation, Severe	1
Mental Retardation, Profound	1
Reactive Behavior Disorder + Mental Retardation, Moderate	1
Total	7

Hearing Severe, Visual Severe, Neurological, Cardiac

Mental Retardation, Severe	2
Mental Retardation, Profound	2
Mental Retardation, Severe + Autism	1
Mental Retardation, Moderate + Partial Syndrome of Autism	1
Total	6

Appendix B

Areas of Behavioral Disturbance, with Examples

Sleep—Makes a fuss while being put to sleep; falls asleep with difficulty; awakens several times during the night, comes into parents' room, and is found in the morning sleeping on floor next to their bed; insists on sleeping with parent; sleeps most of time, awakening only to eat; refuses to stay in bed.

Feeding—Picky eater; eats only soft mushy foods; dawdles; does not feed self; drinks only from bottle; eats very small amount; will not eat meat; leaves table when does not like smell of food; takes all food in bottle; cannot swallow solids; goes on food binges; refuses to use utensils—will only finger feed; will not eat sitting down.

Dressing—Refuses to dress himself; undresses at inappropriate times; uncooperative; gets annoyed easily with dressing procedure; refuses to change to seasonal clothing; very fussy about textures.

Elimination—Wets self frequently during day or night; soils pants; refuses to use toilet—hides behind curtains to have bowel movement.

Mood—Has temper tantrums; shows no variation in mood expression; behaves oppositionally; withdraws from people; shows flattened affect; has infantile affective behavior; wears a silly grin; screams without provocation; has vacant expression.

Discipline—Shows extreme persistence in getting own way; refuses to cooperate with ordinary requests; stubborn; has to be restrained physically when his activity is socially out of place; cannot be trained not to engage in dangerous acts; is difficult to train regarding daily routines; doesn't listen when spoken to; is destructive. Examples of destructiveness included tearing books, breaking lamps, emptying drawers, turning over furniture, throwing objects on the floor, breaking toys.

Motor Activity—Runs rather than walks; runs or walks purposelessly; frantically touches objects; moves constantly in slow motion; waddles when walks, has unsteady gait and poor balance; has shuffling gait; crawls as only means of locomotion; everts feet when walking; walks into objects, walls, and people.

Habits and Rituals—Twirls objects round and round in front of eyes; mouths objects; chews paint, soap, deodorant, paper, laces, matches, metallic objects, etc.; spins in circles; hangs with head down on side of bed for hours; plucks eyelids, pushes finger in eye; gazes at lights; plays with fingers in front of light; touches everything and everybody; smells everything; grinds teeth; hits face; opens and closes hands for long periods of time; bangs head; rocks back and forth; rolls head from side to side; stares at shiny surfaces.

Somatic—Drools; shakes and becomes tremulous when nervous; vomits or gags with unpleasant odors.

Speech—No speech; speech below age expectancy; non-communicative sounds; deviations of intonation; poor articulation; infantile quality of articulation; echolalia, immediate or delayed; explosive sounds.

Social Relationships—Prefers to play alone; does not play with children; overdependent, clings to mother; fights against being cuddled or kissed; oblivious to surroundings and examiner in testing situation; avoids eye contact; bossy with children; becomes anxious when separated from parents; does not interact with adults or children; demands excessive attention; screams with new people; aggressive. (Examples of aggressive behavior in social relationships: hits, kicks, and bites in anger; pulls people's hair; hits children; teases; hostile behavior; makes threatening gestures to people; pushes and hits strangers; picks fights with anybody; grabs from siblings.)

Learning—General difficulty in learning; has highly selective attention span; has poor retention of what he learns; does not cooperate when attempt is made to teach; does not learn specific gestures for social situations.

Other Behavioral Deviations—The behaviors which did not fit clearly into the 12 categories illustrated above were placed here under three sub-headings:

   a) Non-specific immaturity: Behaves like a much younger child; uses toys inappropriately or drops them to floor in infantile manner.
   b) Is afraid of animals, thunder, cars, darkness, noise, crowds, getting clothes dirty, motion play, doctors.
   c) Additional problems: short attention span; unusually high threshold to pain or temperature; perseveration; very distractible; writes from right to left.

REFERENCES

ALFORD, C. A. JR., NEVA, F. A., and WELLER, T. H., 1964, Virologic and Serologic Studies on Human Products of Conception after Maternal Rubella, *New England Journal of Medicine*, 271: 1275-1281.

AMERICAN PSYCHIATRIC ASSOCIATION, 1968, *Diagnostic and Statistical Manual of Mental Disorders, II*. Washington, D.C.: American Psychiatric Association.

AVERY, G. B., MONIF, G. R. G., SEVER, J. L., and LEIKIN, S. L., 1965, Rubella Syndrome after Inapparent Maternal Illness, *American Journal of Diseases of Children*, 110: 444-446.

BENDER, L., 1970, The Life Course of Children with Autism and Mental Retardation. In Menolascino, F. J. (Ed.), *Psychiatric Approaches to Mental Retardation*. New York: Basic Books.

BINDON, D. M., 1957, Personality Characteristics of Rubella Deaf Children: Implications for Teaching of the Deaf in General, *American Annals of the Deaf*, 102: 264-270.

167

BIRCH, H. G. (Ed.), 1964, *Brain Damage in Children.* Baltimore: Williams & Wilkins.

BLATTNER, R. J., 1966, Congenital Rubella: Persistent Infection of the Brain and Liver, *Journal of Pediatrics,* 68: 997-999.

BORTNER, M. and BIRCH, H. G., 1970, Cognitive Capacity and Cognitive Competence, *American Journal of Mental Deficiency,* 74: 735-744.

BRITISH MEDICAL JOURNAL, 1965, editorial, New Rubella Syndrome, 2: 1382-1383.

BUTLER, N. R., DUDGEON, J. A., HAYES, K., PECKHAM, C. S., and WYBAR, K., 1965, Persistence of Rubella Antibody with and without Embryopathy, *British Medical Journal,* 2: 1027-1029.

CAIN, L. F., LEVINE, L., and ELZEY, F. F., 1963, *Cain-Levine Social Competency Scale.* Palo Alto: Consulting Psychological Press.

CATTELL, P., 1960, *The Measurement of Intelligence of Infants and Young Children.* New York: Psychological Corporation.

CHESS, S., 1969, *An Introduction to Child Psychiatry.* New York: Grune and Stratton.

CHESS, S. and HASSIBI, M., 1970, Behavior Deviations in Mentally Retarded Children, *Journal of the American Academy of Child Psychiatry,* 9: 282-297.

CHESS, S. and KORN, S., 1970, Temperament and Behavior Disorders in Mentally Retarded Children, *Archives of General Psychiatry,* 23: 122-130.

COOPER, L. Z., GREEN, R. H., KRUGMAN, S., GILES, J. P., and MIRICK, G. S., 1965, Neonatal Thrombocytopenic Purpura and Other Manifestations of Rubella Contracted in Utero, *American Journal of Diseases of Children,* 110: 416-427.

COOPER, L. Z. and KRUGMAN, S., 1966, Diagnosis and Management: Congenital Rubella, *Pediatrics,* 37: 335-338.

COOPER, L. Z., ZIRING, P. R., OCKERSE, A. B., FEDUN, B. A., KIELY, B., and KRUGMAN, S., 1969, Rubella: Clinical Manifestations and Management, *American Journal of Diseases of Children,* 118: 18-29.

CREAK, M., 1961, Schizophrenic Syndrome in Childhood: Progress Report of a Working Party, *Cerebral Palsy Bulletin,* 3: 501-504.

DEKABAN, A. and O'ROURKE, J., 1958, Abnormalities in Offspring Related to Maternal Rubella During Pregnancy, *Neurology,* 8: 387-392.

DESMOND, M. M., WILSON, G. S., MELNICK, J. L., SINGER, D. B., ZION, T. E., RUDOLPH, A. J., PINEDA, R. G., ZIAI, M. H., and BLATTNER,

R. J., 1967, Congenital Rubella Encephalitis, *Journal of Pediatrics*, 71: 311-331.

DESMOND, M. M., WILSON, G. S., VERNIAUD, W. M., MELNICK, J. L., and RAWLS, W. E., 1970, The Early Growth and Development of Infants with Congenital Rubella. In *Advances in Teratology*, Volume IV. New York: Academic Press.

DOLL, E. A., 1953, *The Measurement of Social Competence: A Manual for the Vineland Social Maturity Scale*. Minneapolis: Educational Test Publishers.

DUDGEON, J. A., 1969, Congenital Rubella: Pathogenesis and Immunology, *American Journal of Diseases of Children*, 118: 35-44.

ELKIND, D., 1967, Cognition in Infancy and Early Childhood. In Brackbill, Y. (Ed.), *Infancy and Early Childhood*. New York: The Free Press.

FORBES, J. A., 1969, Rubella: Historical Aspects, *American Journal of Diseases of Children*, 118: 5-11.

FREEDMAN, D. A., FOX-KOLENDA, B. J., and BROWN, S. L., 1970, A Multihandicapped Rubella Baby: The First 18 Months, *Journal of the American Academy of Child Psychiatry*, 9: 298-317.

GRAHAM, P. and RUTTER, M., 1968, Organic Brain Dysfunction and Child Psychiatric Disorder, *British Medical Journal*, 3: 695-700.

GREGG, N. M., 1941, Congenital Cataract Following German Measles in the Mother, *Transactions of the Ophthalmological Society of Australia*, 3: 35-46.

GREGG, N., 1945, Rubella During Pregnancy of the Mother, with Its Sequelae of Congenital Defects in the Child, *Medical Journal of Australia*, 1: 313-315.

GUBBAY, S. S., LOBASCHER, M., and KINGERLEE, P., 1970, A Neurological Appraisal of Autistic Children: Results of a Western Australian Survey, *Developmental Medicine and Child Neurology*, 12: 422-429.

HARDY, J. B., MONIF, G. R. G., and SEVER, J. L., 1966, Studies in Congenital Rubella, Baltimore, 1964-65: Clinical and Virologic, *Bulletin of the Johns Hopkins Hospital*, 118: 97-108.

HARDY, J. B., McCRACKEN, G. H. JR., GILKESON, M. R., and SEVER, J. L., 1969, Adverse Fetal Outcome Following Maternal Rubella after the First Trimester of Pregnancy, *Journal of the American Medical Association*, 207: 2414-2420.

HEGGIE, A. D. and WEIR, W. C., 1964, Isolation of Rubella Virus from a Mother and Fetus, *Pediatrics*, 34: 278-280.

HICKS, D. E., 1970, Comparison Profiles of Rubella and Non-Rubella Deaf Children, *American Annals of the Deaf*, 115: 86-92.

HORSTMANN, D. M., BANATVALA, J. E., RIORDAN, J. T., PAYNE, M. C., WHITTEMORE, R., OPTON, E. M., and FLOREY, C. DUVE., 1965, Maternal Rubella and the Rubella Syndrome in Infants, *American Journal of Diseases of Children*, 110: 408-415.

HUNT, J. McV., 1961, *Intelligence and Experience*. New York: The Ronald Press.

JACKSON, A. D. M. and FISCH, J., 1958, Deafness Following Maternal Rubella: Results of a Prospective Investigation, *Lancet*, 2: 1241-1244.

KANNER, L., 1943, Autistic Disturbances in Affective Contact, *Nervous Child*, 2: 217-250.

KAY, H. E. M., PEPPERCORN, M. E., PORTERFIELD, J. S., McCARTHY, K., and TAYLOR-ROBINSON, C. H., 1964, Congenital Rubella Infection of a Human Embryo, *British Medical Journal*, 2: 166-167.

KIRMAN, B. H., 1955, Rubella as a Cause of Mental Deficiency, *Lancet*, 2: 1113-1115.

KORONES, S. B., AINGER, L. E., MONIF, G. R. G., ROANE, J., SEVER, J. L., and FUSTE, F., 1967, Congenital Rubella Syndrome: New Clinical Aspects with Recovery of Virus from Affected Infants, *Journal of Pediatrics*, 67: 166-181.

KRUGMAN, S., 1965, Rubella—New Light On an Old Disease, *Journal of Pediatrics*, 67: 159-161.

LAMBERT, H. P., STERN, H., and WELLSTEED, A. J., 1965, Congenital Rubella Syndrome, *Lancet*, 11: 826-827.

LELAND, H., CHELLHAUS, M., NIHIRA, K., and FOSTER, R., 1967, Adaptive Behavior: A New Direction in the Classification of the Mentally Retarded, *Mental Retardation Abstracts*, 4: 359-387.

LEVINE, E. S., 1951, Psychoeducational Study of Children Born Deaf Following Maternal Rubella in Pregnancy, *American Journal of Diseases of Children*, 81: 627-635.

LEWIS, M. M., 1957, Language Perception and Reasoning. In Erving, A. (Ed.), *The Modern Educational Treatment of Deafness*. Manchester: Manchester University Press.

LINDQUIST, J. M., PLOTKIN, S. A., SHAW, L., GILDEN, R. V., and WILLIAMS, M. L., 1965, Congenital Rubella Syndrome as a Systemic Infection: Studies of Affected Infants Born in Philadelphia, U.S.A., *British Medical Journal*, 2: 1401-1406.

LOTTER, V., 1966, Services for a Group of Autistic Children in Middlesex. In Wing, J. K. (Ed.), *Early Childhood Autism*. Oxford: Pergamon Press.

LUNDSTROM, R., 1962, Rubella During Pregnancy: A Follow-Up Study of Children Born after an Epidemic of Rubella in Sweden, 1951, with Additional Investigations on Prophylaxis and Treatment of Maternal Rubella, *Acta Paediatrica*, 51: Supplement 133.

LUNDSTROM, R. and AHNSJO, S., 1962, Mental Development Following Maternal Rubella: A Follow-Up Study of Children Born in 1951-52, *Acta Paediatrica*, 51: Supplement 135: 153-159.

MENSER, M. A., DODS, L., and HARLEY, J. D., 1967, A Twenty-five Year Follow-Up of Congenital Rubella, *Lancet*, 2: 1347-1350.

MICHAELS, R. H. and KENNY, F. M., 1969, Postnatal Growth Retardation in Congenital Rubella, *Pediatrics*, 43: 251-259.

MONIF, G. R. G., HARDY, J. B., and SEVER, J. L., 1966, Studies in Congenital Rubella, Baltimore, 1964-65: Epidemiologic and Virologic, *Bulletin of the Johns Hopkins Hospital*, 118: 85-96.

NATIONAL CENTER FOR HEALTH STATISTICS, 1967, *Vital Statistics of the United States, 1965*. Washington, D.C.: U.S. Government Printing Office.

PARKMAN, P. D., BUESCHER, E. L., and ARTENSTEIN, M. S., 1962, Recovery of Rubella Virus from Army Recruits, *Proceedings of the Society for Experimental Biology and Medicine*, 111: 225-230.

PHILLIPS, C. A., MELNICK, J. L., YOW, M. D., BAYATPOUR, M., and BURKHARDT, M., 1965, Persistence of Virus in Infants with Congenital Rubella and in Normal Infants with a History of Maternal Rubella, *Journal of the American Medical Association*, 193: 1027-1029.

PIAGET, J., 1952, *The Origins of Intelligence in Children*. New York: International Universities Press.

PLOTKIN, S. A., OSKI, F. A., HARTNETT, E. M., HERVADA, A. R., FRIEDMAN, S., and GOWING, J., 1967, Some Recently Recognized Manifestations of the Rubella Syndrome, *Journal of Pediatrics*, 67: 182-191.

POND, D. A., 1961, Psychiatric Aspects of Epileptic and Brain-Damaged Children, *British Medical Journal*, 5265: 1454.

RAINER, J. D., ALTSHULER, K. Z., and KALLMAN, F. S., (Eds.), 1969, *Family and Mental Health Problems in a Deaf Population*. Springfield, Ill.: Charles C Thomas.

RIMLAND, B., 1964, *Infantile Autism*. New York: Appleton-Century-Crofts.

RUSSELL, B., 1921, *The Analysis of Mind.* London: Allen and Unwin.
RUTTER, M., 1966, Personal Communication, cited in Wing, J. K. (Ed.), *Early Childhood Autism.* Oxford: Pergamon Press.
RUTTER, M., 1968, Concepts of Autism: A Review of Research, *Journal of Child Psychology and Psychiatry,* 9: 1-25.
SEVER, J. L., HARDY, J. B., NELSON, K. B., and GILKESON, M. R., 1969, Rubella in the Collaborative Perinatal Research Study, *American Journal of Diseases of Children,* 118: 123-132.
SHERIDAN, M. D., 1964, Final Report of a Prospective Study of Children Whose Mothers Had Rubella in Early Pregnancy, *British Medical Journal,* 2: 536-539.
SINGER, D. B., RUDOLPH, A. J., ROSENBERG, H. S., RAWLS, W. E., and BONIUK, M., 1967, Pathology of the Congenital Rubella Syndrome, *Journal of Pediatrics,* 71: 665-675.
SPIKER, C. C., 1966, The Concept of Development: Relevant and Irrelevant Issues, *Monographs of the Society for Research in Child Development,* Serial No. 107, Vol. 31, No. 5.
STRAUSS, A. A. and WERNER, H., 1941, The Mental Organization of the Brain-Injured Child, *American Journal of Psychiatry,* 97: 1194.
SWAN, C., TOSTEVIN, A. L., MOORE, B., MAYO, H., and BLACK, G. H. B., 1943, Congenital Defects in Infants Following Infectious Diseases During Pregnancy, *Medical Journal of Australia,* 2: 201-210.
TERMAN, L. M., 1916, *The Measurement of Intelligence.* Boston: Houghton Mifflin.
TERMAN, L. M. and MERRILL, M., 1960, *Stanford-Binet Intelligence Scale, Manual for the Third Revision: Form L-M.* Boston: Houghton Mifflin.
THOMAS, A., CHESS, S., and BIRCH, H. G., 1968, *Temperament and Behavior Disorders in Children.* New York: New York University Press.
THOMAS, A., CHESS, S., BIRCH, H. G., HERTZIG, M. E., and KORN, S., 1963, *Behavioral Individuality in Early Childhood.* New York: New York University Press.
TREFFERT, D. A., 1970, Epidemiology of Infantile Autism, *Archives of General Psychiatry,* 22: 431-438.
TONDURY, G. and SMITH, D. W., 1966, Fetal Rubella Pathology, *Journal of Pediatrics,* 68: 867-879.
VERNON, McC., 1967, Characteristics Associated with Post-Rubella Deaf Children: Psychological, Educational and Physical, *Volta Review,* 69: 176-185.

VERNON, McC., 1969, *Multiply Handicapped Deaf Children: Medical, Educational and Psychological Considerations*. Washington, D.C.: Council for Exceptional Children.

WEINBERGER, M. M., MASLAND, M. W., ASBED, R-A., and SEVER, J. L., 1970, Congenital Rubella Presenting as Retarded Language Development, *American Journal of Diseases of Children*, 120: 125-128.

WELLER, T. H. and NEVA, F. A., 1962, Propagation in Tissue Culture of Cytopathic Agents from Patients with Rubella-like Illness, *Proceedings of the Society for Experimental Biology and Medicine*, 111: 215-225.

WEST, C., 1881, Presidential Summary, *Transactions of the International Congress of Medicine*, 4: 34.

WHITE, L. R., SEVER, J. L., and ALEPA, F. P., 1969, Maternal and Congenital Rubella Before 1964: Frequency, Clinical Features and Search for Isoimmune Phenomena, *Journal of Pediatrics*, 74: 198-207.

WILLIAMS, K. E., 1970, Some Psychiatric Observations in a Group of Maladjusted Deaf Children, *Journal of Child Psychology and Psychiatry*, 11: 1-18.

WRIGHT, H. T., 1971, Prenatal Factors in Causation (Viral). In Koch, R. and Dobson, J. C. (Eds.), *The Mentally Retarded Child and His Family*. New York: Brunner/Mazel.

Index